This book is dedicated to Barack Obama,
who should know better.

The Teachers We Need vs. the Teachers We Have

Realities and Possibilities

Lawrence Baines

ROWMAN & LITTLEFIELD EDUCATION
A division of
ROWMAN & LITTLEFIELD PUBLISHERS, INC.
Lanham • New York • Toronto • Plymouth, UK

Published by Rowman & Littlefield Education
A division of Rowman & Littlefield Publishers, Inc.
A wholly owned subsidiary of
The Rowman & Littlefield Publishing Group, Inc.
4501 Forbes Boulevard, Suite 200, Lanham, Maryland 20706
http://www.rowmaneducation.com

Estover Road, Plymouth PL6 7PY, United Kingdom

*Special thanks to my research assistants, Cynthia Rundquist and Courtney
Krieger, for their immense help.*

British Library Cataloguing in Publication Information Available

Library of Congress Cataloging-in-Publication Data

Baines, Lawrence.
   The teachers we need vs. the teachers we have : the realities and the
possibilities / Lawrence Baines.
      p. cm.
   Includes bibliographical references.
   ISBN 978-1-60709-701-3 (cloth : alk. paper) — ISBN 978-1-60709-702-0
(pbk. : alk. paper) — ISBN 978-1-60709-703-7 (electronic)
   1. Teachers—Certification—United States. 2. Teachers—Training of—
United States. I. Title.
   LB1771.B35 2010
   379.1'57—dc22

2009050521

∞ ™ The paper used in this publication meets the minimum requirements of
American National Standard for Information Sciences—Permanence of
Paper for Printed Library Materials, ANSI/NISO Z39.48-1992.

Printed in the United States of America

Contents

Chapter One

The Rise of the Test

It is instructive to note that, until relatively recently, proof of a teacher's competence consisted of the completion of a degree program in education at a university or college. The testing of teachers was considered as early as the 1960s, but few states required a test for certification at that time.

However, after *A Nation at Risk* (National Commission on Excellence in Education 1984) laid the blame for faltering American ingenuity on the mediocre achievement levels of students in math and science in public schools, the teacher-testing movement gained real momentum. By 1985, more than half the states began requiring a passing score on an exam. Further reforms focused on the preparation of elementary teachers, with state governments drafting new laws requiring significantly more hours in mathematics and science.

During the 1980s, so deep was the disdain for teacher preparation that degrees in education were perfunctorily abolished. Even teachers of very young children were required to have a major in a content area other than education. The prejudice against a major in education has only become more entrenched over time.

Of all the states in the union, only North Dakota still requires future teachers to major in education; the other forty-nine states allow future teachers to choose any major *except* education. As a result, future first-grade teachers are taking more courses in postmodern rhetoric and calculus and fewer courses in child development and instructional strategies.

I was an English teacher in Texas during the 1980s, and among the first wave of teachers ever mandated to sit for a competency exam. At the time that the governor of Texas promised slight raises for teachers, he also pledged that all teachers would take competency tests.

Although I had already graduated with honors from the University of Texas at Austin; had been issued a lifetime certificate by the state of Texas to teach English, journalism, reading, and computer literacy; had completed a master's degree in business computer systems; and had taught five years, I was required, along with all other teachers in the state, to take a test to retain the right to teach.

The school where I taught had no auditorium and the gym was not air conditioned, so one hot Saturday morning in May, all of us gathered in the cafeteria to take the test, then called the TECAT (Texas Exam of the Competency of Administrators and Teachers). The time allotted for completion of the exam was several hours, but I finished it in about forty-five minutes—not because I was particularly brilliant, but because the test was constructed at a level of difficulty that would not tax a seventh grader.

Ultimately, Texas teachers received modest raises, and the TECAT, which was created and administered at a cost of several million dollars, screened out less than one-half of 1 percent of Texas's teachers. When the governor of Texas asserted that anyone who failed TECAT did not deserve to be a teacher, he was referring to only a handful of individuals. Every few years since the administration of the TECAT, the state of Texas has routinely announced a new test with a new acronym, issued fresh platitudes about the increased level of difficulty of the test, and offered further exhortations concerning the quality of teachers.

A CACOPHONY OF TESTING

Since the 1980s, most states have followed Texas's lead and established requirements for elaborate testing of teachers. Today, prospective teachers in forty-seven states must pass a competency test of some sort, usually in the content area. The holdout states, Nebraska, Montana, and Iowa, still use the evidence of a four-year university degree, rather than a test, as an indication of teacher competency.

However, in an odd reprise of the old worries over the teaching of mathematics and science in the elementary grades, in 2006 the federal government stepped in and demanded that Iowa require competency exams. However, these tests of competency were not required of middle or secondary teachers—only of graduates from elementary education programs.

Originally, states constructed their own exams, but gradually departments of education got out of the testing business and outsourced these duties to testing companies such as Educational Testing Service (ETS) and National Evaluation Service (NES). ETS offers what has become a sort of de facto national battery of exams for teachers.

The PRAXIS I, a basic competency test, is used as an entrance requirement for admission to many teacher-education programs. PRAXIS II, which may consist of several tests, including content knowledge, teacher practice, and writing competency, serves as the gateway to initial certification. (When forced to choose a test, Iowa chose PRAXIS II for its elementary teachers.) PRAXIS III is a classroom-observation assessment in which a probationary teacher is evaluated on his or her suitability for full, professional certification. PRAXIS III, the least-subscribed test in ETS's battery of tests and most performance-based, is currently undergoing revision.

States that wished to have more of a state-centric exam used to outsource their business to NES, who supposedly "customized" exams according to the whims of each state. In 2006, NES was acquired by the publishing conglomerate Pearson. Now NES is called the Evaluation Systems group of Pearson. While the PRAXIS series remains the most common assessment among states, with thirty-six states using PRAXIS II, Pearson has built a significant following, with nine states.

Rhode Island uses the PRAXIS II PLT (Principles of Learning and Teaching), but requires no PRAXIS II content-area exams, except for elementary teachers. Some states, such as Colorado, allow students to take either the PLACE (Program for Licensing Assessments for Colorado's Educators; created by Pearson) or PRAXIS II (from ETS). Florida is the only state that still constructs and uses its own tests.

One of the oddities of teacher testing in the United States is the radical difference in acceptable passing scores among states. Although states may use identical tests, passing scores vary widely. For example, a score of 142 on the PRAXIS II is considered sufficient to demonstrate mastery of content in English in Washington, D.C., but a 142 is considered inadequate anywhere else in the country. Thirty more points, or a score of 172, is required to teach English in Virginia, Connecticut, and Vermont.

Pearson's tests are usually normalized so that the cutoff score is around 240, though New York uses a modified Pearson test whose cutoff score is 220.

THE EFFECTIVENESS OF TEACHER TESTING

One would assume, because teacher testing has proliferated across the United States for more than twenty-five years at the cost of billions of dollars, that there would be ample evidence substantiating testing as an effective method of insuring teacher quality. In fact, what a teacher scores on a test has little correlation to their effectiveness in the classroom (Goldhaber 2007).

The good news on standardized testing is that the math scores of elementary-age children have escalated some twenty points since 1985. Some pro-test advocates consider this to be confirmation of the power of teacher testing. Of course, to claim that the rise in mathematics achievement of fourth graders is attributable more to a teacher exam rather than to a revised elementary curriculum jammed with substantially more mathematics seems dubious. The power is likely not in a standardized test for teachers, but in the curriculum delivered to students.

Clotfelter, Ladd, and Vigdor (2006) reported on one of the few studies that actually found a positive relationship between teacher test scores and students' test scores, though the correlation they uncovered was miniscule. For example, for the correlation to be present at all, a comparison would have to involve teachers at opposite ends of the spectrum—one teacher would have to be among the highest scoring in the nation and the other would have to be among the lowest scoring in the nation.

Even when these two extremes are used, the mean difference in student achievement attributable to testing would be perhaps one point on a one-hundred-point exam. In a large study of the impact of increased teacher testing, Angrist and Guryan found "no evidence of a corresponding increase in [teacher] quality" (2008, 483).

Texas, now with more than two decades of teacher-testing experience and countless millions in state monies spent, can proclaim that the achievement of its students remains solidly in the bottom third of the nation, at least according to tests of the National Assessment of Educational Progress (NAEP). Indeed, one of the epiphanies gleaned from a close examination of teacher testing across states is that many of the states that require the most tests consistently post the lowest achievement scores.

For example, table 1.1 compares trends in student achievement in reading among thirteen-year-olds in Texas, a state that tests teachers fre-

Table 1.1. Trends in Reading Achievement among 13-Year-Olds in Texas and Montana

State	Reading Score 13-year-olds 1998	Reading Score 13-year-olds 2007	Gain
Texas	262	261	−1
Montana	270	271	+1

Note: Achievement as measured by National Assessment of Educational Progress (NAEP) reading scores.

quently, with thirteen-year-olds from Montana, a state that uses no teacher tests.

Obviously, a comparison of NAEP reading scores in Texas and Montana from 1998 to 2007 indicates little correlation between student gains in achievement and increased levels of teacher testing.

TESTING AND EXPERIENCE

Originally, teacher tests in the content area were thought to be supplemental to preparation at the university, which included courses in content-area instruction, educational psychology, special education, and student teaching. At one time, state laws related to teacher certification emphasized that prospective teachers must be knowledgeable in both pedagogy and content, and have at least some experience working with children before entering a classroom as a full-time instructor-of-record.

Since 2000, state laws concerning teacher quality have been revised again and again to better accommodate alternative certification providers, whose programs routinely eschew both academic preparation and field experience. As a result, statutes mandating adequate preparation in pedagogy and explicating minimum requirements for practice teaching prior to certification are no longer enforced.

Increasingly in the United States today, the sole requirement for entering the teaching profession has become a passing score on a content-area exam. The popular alternative certification program Teach For America, which has grown exponentially over the past few years, requires only a bachelor's degree, a test score, and five weeks crammed with information on "how to teach."

The American Board for Certification of Teacher Excellence (ABCTE) has managed to convince legislators in nine states—Florida, Idaho, Mississippi, Missouri, New Hampshire, Pennsylvania, South Carolina, Utah, and Oklahoma—to revise state law to allow a passing score on the ABCTE exam to be the sole requirement for teacher certification. On the ABCTE exam, candidates need only guess correctly on about half of the multiple-choice questions to earn a passing mark.

No courses in content, pedagogy, psychology, or foundations are required. No field experience and no student teaching. Prospective teachers pay the ABCTE a few hundred dollars, flip through a few webpages, take an online test, and presto! They are certified teachers.

Accounting and law use tests heavy on technical knowledge as a way to insure a minimum level of competency among workers. The process of becoming a certified public accountant is grueling and rigorous as is the process for becoming a licensed lawyer. Unlike teaching, both accounting and law have professional organizations that exert control over the process of becoming licensed.

Both accounting and law require candidates to enroll in subject-specific, postbaccalaureate programs at accredited institutions. Once candidates complete their academic course work, they become apprentices in the field and are expected to pass an exam to gain entry into the profession. Although law and accounting can be highly technical, all three components—academic course work, fieldwork, and a passing score on an exam—are required.

To become a teacher in most states today, absolutely no training is required—the only requirements are a bachelor's degree (in anything) and a passing score on a content exam. Unlike law and accounting, the test for teachers is not one that has been approved by the profession. For example, the ABCTE creates and scores their own tests, without regard to standards, the objections of school administrators, and denunciations by professional organizations.

If the ABCTE were training lawyers, an aspiring lawyer would not have to go to law school, would not have to take the bar exam, and would not have to engage in any sort of training. Instead, future lawyers could go online to take a test, get half of the answers correct, and instantly become a member of the bar.

The argument can be made that, while teaching may involve some technical knowledge, it is more of a performance-oriented profession, and more similar to athletics, music, sociology, and police work than to technical fields (Levine 2006). Like police officers, teachers must learn to work with a variety of constituents, young and old; must learn how to break up fights; must know how to work with colleagues and administrators to solve complex problems; must be able to identify danger and protect the innocent; and must be able to communicate effectively with their intended audiences.

To acquire competency as a policeman or policewoman, cadets take a full slate of academic course work, but they also engage in a variety of simulations, several different kinds of fieldwork, and finally, extended internships under the guidance of veteran officers. Only after successfully completing each step of the process does a cadet become a full-fledged officer.

But more and more states are replacing high expectations for teacher preparation with nothing more than a passing score on content-area tests—tests that have no proven validity, tests that have shown no correlation to student performance. If police officers were trained like teachers, cadets would take a test one day and be out walking the streets with a loaded weapon the next day.

Consider the differences in the preparation programs of police officers and the preparation programs for teachers. One profession works primarily with lawbreakers and evildoers. This profession requires academic preparation specific to the responsibilities and duties of the position and rigorous, field-based training.

The other profession works with children. The profession that works with children requires no academic preparation and no training. Instead, all that is required to work with children in many states is a passing score on a multiple-choice test.

CONCLUSION

For better or worse, testing has become part of the accepted training regimen for prospective teachers in the United States today. Recently, the emphasis on teacher-competency tests has shifted from expertise in pedagogy and diverse classroom experiences to knowledge of content. As a result in many states, the only nonnegotiable aspect of teacher training has become a passing score on a content-area exam. As the push for content-area tests has grown stronger, requirements for course work in pedagogy, knowledge of child development, and experience working with children have diminished or disappeared completely.

Although forty-seven states require teachers to pass a content-area test, what constitutes a passing score varies from state to state. Most states require the PRAXIS II content-area exam, though some states use "customized" tests created by Pearson. Florida is the only state that still creates and assesses its own teacher-competency exam.

Chapter Two

Trends in Alternative Certification

Washington, D.C., is emblematic of the current state of confusion over alternative teacher-preparation in the United States. According to the website of Washington, D.C., schools and its Title II Report for the past three years, the city has no alternative certification programs. Yet in the 2008 Title II Report, American University, which is located in Washington, D.C., notes that 113 students were seeking alternative licensure through its programs (U.S. Department of Education 2009c).

In addition to alternative programs run through universities, Teach For America (2009) claims "a corps of 290 of the nation's top recent college graduates . . . working in underserved schools across the D.C. Region." Teach For America's claim of 290 graduates would make it the largest certification program in Washington, D.C., by a significant margin. However, according to the Office of the State Superintendent of Education Office of Educator Licensing and Accreditation (2008), Teach For America is not an approved certification program for the District of Columbia.

If the situation in Washington, D.C., were not sufficiently baffling, consider the following passage from D.C.'s 2008 Title II Report (U.S. Department of Education 2009c):

> While the District of Columbia's State Education Agency has not created and implemented specific alternative route teacher prep programs, it recognizes alternative route program completers and has adopted the federal definition of an alternate route program. Specifically, the District of Columbia considers an individual who is completing his/her teacher preparation while also serving as the teacher of record as participating in an alternate route to certification. The 7 institutions which prepare teachers for licensure in DC

use their discretion to determine whether they will accept alternative route candidates.

In other words, an individual who happens to find themselves being paid as a teacher in Washington, D.C., is automatically en route to becoming alternatively certified. Being that this policy emanates from a locality that professes to have no alternative certification program, the District of Columbia's policies on certification are as clear as mud.

Perhaps one reason for Washington, D.C.'s confusion is that it chose to meet the demand for the highly qualified teachers required by the No Child Left Behind Act by simply altering the definition of *highly qualified*. Instead of requiring prospective teachers to obtain certification prior to employment, D.C. schools required only passing scores on PRAXIS I and PRAXIS II.

In this manner, those wanting to teach who had never taught and who had never taken any courses in how to teach were miraculously elevated to the realms of the "highly qualified." While it is justifiable to blast D.C.'s shoddy standards, the truth is that the certification process for teachers in most states is similar—or worse. Through such linguistic tinkering, *highly qualified*, originally conceived as a seal of teacher quality, has lost all credibility.

Originally, alternative certification was a stopgap to fill a vacancy with an unqualified individual when no certified teacher could be found. For example, if a teacher of physics in a rural area of Iowa might have health problems and be forced to take a leave of absence in the middle of the school year, the only way to replace him or her might be to offer the job to an unqualified substitute until a permanent, certified replacement could be found.

Today, alternative certification is no longer alternative—it is mainstream, and the number of alternatively certified teachers is soaring. Forty-seven states have opened their gates to various brands of alternative certification, even states with low or negative population-growth rates and large teacher surpluses such as Vermont, Pennsylvania, Maine, Wisconsin, and Ohio. Recently, Secretary of Education Arne Duncan characterized alternative certification as an attractive alternative route for prospective teachers (Medina 2009).

During the 1980s, in response to public sentiment and heavy legislative intervention, most colleges of education revamped programs so that prospective teachers had to take, at a minimum, the same number of courses as majors who were not going to be teachers. Initiatives included extending the time students were required to teach in schools, and demanding more preparation in teaching in the certification area.

At the same time that the front door to teacher education was being made more difficult for entry, state legislatures began opening the back door to certification ever wider through increasingly quick-and-easy routes to certification. However, characterizing all alternative programs as "quick and easy" would be wrong because some alternative programs are decent, or even good. Indeed, some university-based, multiyear, field-intensive graduate programs call themselves "alternative," though they share no similarities with quick-and-easy, corporate-run programs in the same state.

Frankly, many alternative programs do nothing to prepare teachers—they offer no courses, provide no opportunities for practice teaching, and require no internship. Instead, they confer certification for a fee. An example of the disparities among alternative programs is evident in the state of Alabama, whose bifurcated system of teacher certification is representative of many across the country.

One Alabama alternative program is, in reality, not alternative certification at all but a master of arts in teaching degree, replete with master's level academic courses, extended field hours, and a full semester of student teaching. Another alternative certification program in Alabama is called the Bachelor's Alternative Program (BAP).

It is understandable that the state does not call the degree a bachelor's alternative degree (BAD), though BAD may be a more appropriate acronym than BAP. BAP is bad because students take no course work and have no classroom experience, yet are hired as full-time teachers.

Students enrolled in the alternative certification program of the University of Alabama at Birmingham (UAB) are required to take over seventeen more hours in the content area than students in BAP. In addition, students in UAB's program take four courses in subject-specific methods, while BAP teachers have zero subject-specific methods courses. UAB students are required to take a substantial pre-student-teaching, field-based course as well as a full-semester of student teaching; BAP students have zero field requirements.

BAP students show up in schools the first day with absolutely no experience in the classroom whatsoever. Although BAP students have minimal content-area course work and no classroom experience, they teach a full year without having to take even a basic-skills exam (in Alabama, the basic-skills exam is called the Alabama Prospective Teacher Testing Program, or APTTP). BAP students also have two additional years to pass PRAXIS II.

The more-qualified and better-prepared UAB students must pass both the APTTP and PRAXIS II before setting foot in the classroom. Table 2.1 below compares two of Alabama's alternative programs: alternative certification at UAB, and BAP, which is administered through the state department of education.

When the magna cum laude at UAB and the student completing BAP get hired, they will receive the same pay and benefits. By the end of the second year, the teaching certificate obtained by the graduate of BAP will be indistinguishable from the certificate earned by the magna cum laude. In most states, the teaching certificate would be the indistinguishable *on the first day on the job*.

LEVELS OF QUALITY

One of the oddities shared by all state departments of education in the United States is that certificates are one-size-fits-all. A teacher is either certified or uncertified. One teacher completes work at Stanford University with a 4.0 grade point average and spends three years in urban schools working on becoming a master teacher; a second teacher obtains a baccalaureate degree from the University of Phoenix with a 2.5 grade point average, takes no education courses, avoids all contact with children, and passes a content-area exam.

Both candidates will receive the exact same certificate. To help distinguish among alternative programs in the United States for purposes of quality, it may be useful to classify programs as belonging to one of four categories, based upon the duration and rigor of the preparation.

Level 0: Zilch
Level I: Cram
Level II: Minimal
Level III: Adequate

Table 2.1. Comparison of Two Programs in Alabama: Alternative Certification at the University of Alabama at Birmingham (UAB) and the Bachelor's Alternative Program (BAP)

Name	Hours in Content	Tests	Hours in Education	Hours in Methods of Teaching Content	Pre-Student-Teaching Field Experience	Student Teaching
Bachelor's Alternative Program	32	No tests required to teach; candidates must pass APTTP after first year of teaching, and PRAXIS II at the end of the second year	12 (may be taken via Internet)	0	None	None
University of Alabama at Birmingham, English Education	63	Must pass APTTP and PRAXIS II	19–23	12	3 hours	9–12 hours, full time, 12 weeks
University of Alabama at Birmingham, Math Education	49	Must pass APTTP and PRAXIS II	19–23	12	3 hours	9–12 hours, full time, 12 weeks

The less required of candidates, the lower the level ranking. The more required of candidates, the higher the level ranking. Using this classification system, Alabama's BAP, which requires no field experience and minimal course work, would be Level I: Cram. UAB's alternative program, with its extensive graduate course work and mandated field experiences, would qualify as Level III: Adequate. All of the growth in teacher-certification programs over the past twenty years has been at the two lowest levels: Level 0: Zilch; and Level I: Cram.

As a result, examples of Zilch, Cram, and Minimal programs abound; alternative programs with adequate preparation are rare. To illustrate the wide differences among alternative providers, descriptions of programs in selected states will be provided at each quality level.

Level 0: Zilch

Explanation: Little to no preparation (may include a test required by the state)

Examples:

1. Los Angeles Public Schools
2. The American Board for Certification of Teacher Excellence (ABCTE) in Idaho
3. Alternative 4 and the ABCTE in New Hampshire

Similar programs: Chicago, Milwaukee, Dallas, Houston, New York, Philadelphia, and other large urban school districts have programs much like the district-certification plan in Los Angeles. ABCTE programs have been approved in Florida, Idaho, New Hampshire, Mississippi, Missouri, New Hampshire, South Carolina, Utah, and Oklahoma.

Level 0: Zilch, Example 1: Los Angeles Public Schools

In California, alternative certification is available through universities, businesses, and a wide array of schools. Large urban districts such as the Los Angeles Unified School District (LAUSD) have some of the largest teacher-certification programs in the country (see table 2.2). LAUSD has certified more than eight thousand teachers to date and routinely has more teachers enrolled in certification classes than do universities in the state. Incredibly in California, school districts certify approximately 10 percent of all new teachers, with another 20 percent or so certified through other alternative programs.

As with most urban districts, LAUSD provides the entirety of a prospective teacher's program, including "condensed" courses (if any), mentoring, and assessment. State Bill 57, made law in California in 2001, allows prospective teachers to forgo any training or courses in teacher education whatsoever by taking a test promulgated by Educational Testing Service (ETS), called the Teaching Foundations Test.

The largest traditional teacher-preparation program in California is the mammoth program at National University, which offers all of its programs online. Of course in most states, National's traditional program would be considered alternative. However, in California it is not. National also has a huge alternative program, which requires fewer courses, and it is offered online as well.

Although the disparity between requirements for university-based traditional and Level 0: Zilch alternative programs are vast in most states, in California the two paths are in different galaxies. The University of California at Berkeley's traditional program is at the graduate level and includes a two-year commitment to practice teaching in local schools.

On the other hand, in the program available through LAUSD, candidates begin teaching immediately, though they may have never taken a course in pedagogy or had any previous experience with children. While Berkeley has several gateways that weed out weak or ineffective teachers over the course of two years of study—through course work and field experience in local schools—the program through LAUSD has no gateway. If the candidate in Los Angeles schools somehow survives the first year, then certification is granted.

Level 0: Zilch, Example 2: The American Board for Certification of Teacher Excellence (ABCTE) in Idaho

Idaho only has one level of certification: the standard certificate. However, because the business enterprise ABCTE has entered Idaho, a new interim certificate was developed. The new terminology distinguishes between a *certificate* as temporary and a *credential* as permanent. In other

Table 2.2. Comparison of a Los Angeles Unified School District Program (Level 0: Zilch) with Traditional Programs at the University of California at Berkeley

Name	Tests	Total Hours	Hours in Content	Hours in Education	Hours in Methods of Teaching Content	Pre-Student-Teaching Field Experience	Student Teaching	Other Distinguishing Features
Los Angeles Unified School District, Teacher Certification Early Completion Intern Option	Must pass ETS* subject-area exam within 18 months	0	0	6 (or 240 clock hours) taken before full-time teaching	0	Paid while completing first year of teaching	None	Must pass test and be observed
University of California at Berkeley, English Education (master's program)	Must pass basic skills and ETS subject-area exam	35–43	Must hold a bachelor's degree in English	38	10	Student teaching for two years	15 hours college credit	Student teaching for a full two years; emphasis on multi-culturalism
University of California at Berkeley, Math Education (master's program)	Must pass basic skills and ETS subject-area exam	Varies	54–62	NA	54–62	Student teaching for two years	14 hours college credit	Student teaching for a full two years

*Educational Testing Service, Rosedale Road, Princeton, New Jersey 08541.

states, these terms have completely different meanings. For example in Oklahoma, *certificate* is the term designated for permanent certification, and a temporary certification is called a *license*.

The interim certificate (in Idaho, this is the temporary one) allows ABCTE customers up to three years to complete its program, which is in essence a test-preparation package delivered over the Internet. Online sessions and CD-ROMs have been customized to enable customers to pass the ABCTE exam, which happens to have been created by the ABCTE. The ABCTE also grades the exams. According to the ABCTE's website, most candidates complete the program in ten months or less (American Board for Certification of Teacher Excellence 2009).

As it has in other states, the ABCTE in Idaho sometimes offers one hundred dollars off the regular price of a certificate by having customers write in a "secret code" on the payment form (NEWYEARS100 was the secret code for the coupon that expired February 1, 2009). Students who pass the ABCTE's exams do not have to take PRAXIS II and do not have to student teach.

One wonders how the ABCTE ingratiated itself with Idaho politicians to the extent that it could simultaneously circumvent Idaho law, university preparation, and PRAXIS II. While ABCTE customers are teaching full-time on a full salary with the prospect of full certification in ten months or less, students at Boise State University are expected to take forty-six to forty-nine hours of content, sixteen to thirty-seven hours in education, and twelve hours of teaching methods in the content area as well as to participate in extensive fieldwork, including a sixteen-week stint as student teacher. In addition, students at Boise State must pass PRAXIS II; ABCTE customers are exempt (see table 2.3).

Level 0: Zilch, Example 3: Alternative 4 and the ABCTE in New Hampshire

Quick-and-easy paths to alternative certification flourish in New Hampshire. In July of 2002, the New Hampshire legislature passed a law to address the need for teachers in critical shortage areas throughout the state. According to this law, a local school board, in consultation with the superintendent, may offer a one-time, one-year certificate of eligibility to any person interested in teaching on a full-time or part-time basis.

Table 2.3. Comparison of the ABCTE (Level 0: Zilch) in Idaho with Traditional Programs at Boise State University

Name	Minimum GPA	Hours in Content	Hours in Education	Hours in Methods of Teaching Content	Pre-Student-Teaching Field Experience	Student Teaching	Other Distinguishing Features
ABCTE in Idaho	None	0	0	0	None	None	Offered via online courses and CD-ROM; circumvents PRAXIS II
Boise State, English Education	2.5	49	16	12	yes	16 weeks, full time	Must pass PRAXIS II
Boise State, Math Education	2.75	46	37	12	yes	16 weeks, full time	Must pass PRAXIS II

The legislation includes a provision that allows a district to declare a shortage in a teaching area where a shortage has not been declared by the state.

Incredibly, one route, Alternative 4, allows individuals with as few as six hours in the subject area, no teaching experience, and no preparation to teach in New Hampshire schools at a full salary. With a recommendation from a superintendent and a passing score on PRAXIS II, individuals seeking credentials through Alternative 4 can obtain the highest level of teacher certification (Experienced Educator Certificate) without having to do anything other than show up for work at the local school.

New Hampshire automatically certifies teachers who are nationally certified. Such a policy would seem prudent in relation to those seasoned teachers who participate in the battery of reports, analyses, and exams required by the National Board for Professional Teaching Standards (NB-PTS). However, New Hampshire places customers of the ABCTE in the same category as teachers who have passed the NBPTS.

While ABCTE students are required to guess 50 percent of answers correctly on a multiple-choice test that takes an hour or two, candidates seeking certification through the NBPTS are required to submit work samples, defend their instructional choices, and engage in intensive professional development over the course of several years. Not surprisingly, while many future teachers in New Hampshire are becoming certified through the ABCTE, few are choosing certification through the NBPTS. A grand total of one teacher from New Hampshire became nationally certified through the NBPTS in 2007–2008.

New Hampshire confuses matters by calling its traditional programs *alternatives*. Alternative 1 has to do with in-state teacher-preparation programs, and Alternative 2 has to do with out-of-state teacher-preparation programs or out-of-state alternative programs. The nontraditional paths are alternatives 3A, 3B, 4, and 5. Portfolios are only required for alternatives 3A and 3B, but are also developed to support Alternative 4 and Alternative 5.

Needless to say, neither the logic nor the details of New Hampshire's certification system are easy to understand. Brief descriptions of some of New Hampshire's alternative routes follow.

Alternative 3A: Demonstrated Competencies and Equivalent Experiences This alternative, like Alternative 3B following, is designed for individuals who have gained their teaching skills through means other than those offered by alternatives 1 and 2.

Requirements:

- Bachelor's degree
- Three consecutive months of educational employment
- No grade point average requirement
- No content requirement
- Passing score on PRAXIS I
- Passing score on PRAXIS II (candidates are exempt from PRAXIS I and II if they hold a master's degree in the subject area)
- Submission of a portfolio, and an interview

Alternative 3B: National or Regional Certification   Alternative 3B stipulates that someone who has been nationally certified through the ABCTE or the NBPTS automatically receives certification in New Hampshire.

Requirements:

- No grade point average requirement
- No content requirement
- No passing score on PRAXIS II
- Passing score on the ABCTE exam for ABCTE customers

Alternative 4: Critical Shortage Areas, Career and Technical Education, and Business Administrators   An Individualized Professional Development Plan developed by the school district leads to certification under Alternative 4. The superintendent submits an In Process of Certification Form while the plan is being developed and the basic academic-skills requirement is being met. Under Alternative 4, candidates who passed only two courses in college in the subject area are permitted to teach. Before being awarded the Experienced Educator Certificate (EEC), candidates must pass PRAXIS II and receive a positive recommendation from a superintendent. The fields classified as experiencing a "critical shortage" for 2008–2009 included all fields except social studies and physical education.

Alternative 5: Site-Based Plan Certification Alternative 5 is for candidates who have no teaching experience and no course work in education, but have a job offer. The school district decides on appropriate training (if any) for the candidate.

Requirements:

- Thirty credit hours in the discipline associated with the endorsement, with a 2.5 overall grade point average

To move to full certification (Experienced Educator Certificate), Alternative 5 candidates must meet the following requirements:

- One year successful teaching under a mentor teacher
- Completion of a professional development plan
- Recommendation from the local superintendent of schools

While New Hampshire's alternative programs are at the extreme end of easy, the University of New Hampshire's programs are at the extreme end of tough. Both the mathematics education and English education programs at the University of New Hampshire require a major in the subject area, five years of study, extensive work in schools, several courses in subject-specific teaching methods, and a full-year internship (see table 2.4).

Level I: Cram

Explanation: Course work crammed into five weeks or less, usually without any accompanying classroom experience

Examples:

1. IteachTEXAS and other alternative routes in Texas
2. The ABCTE in Pennsylvania
3. Alternative certification through selected institutions of higher education in Kansas

Similar programs: Teach For America (see chapter 6), corporate-run certification, and Transition to Teaching programs such as Transition to

Table 2.4. Comparison of Alterative 4 (Level 0: Zilch) in New Hampshire with Traditional Programs at the University of New Hampshire

Name	Minimum GPA	Mean SAT Score	Hours in Content	Hours in Education	Field Experience	Student Teaching	Portfolio	Other Distinguishing Features
Alternative 4	None	None	6	0	None	None	None	The professional development plan is at the discretion of the superintendent.
University of New Hampshire, English Education (5-year program)	2.93	1110	120-hour under-graduate degree plus 9–12 hours for postbacc. and portfolio	32	Yes	1 year	Yes	Students complete a baccalaureate degree in English and move into a fifth year of study and full-year internship.
University of New Hampshire, Math Education (5-year program)	2.93	1110	120-hour under-graduate degree plus 9–12 hours for postbacc. and portfolio	32	Yes	1 year	Yes	Students complete a baccalaureate degree in math and move into a fifth year of study and full-year internship.

Teaching at the University of Tennessee at Martin, and the Northern Plains Transition to Teaching program offered by Montana State University at Bozeman

Level I: Cram, Example 1: IteachTEXAS and other alternative routes in Texas

Texas is truly the Wild West of teacher certification with businesses, community colleges, educational service agencies, and school districts routinely doling out more teaching certificates than universities and colleges in the state. The rhetoric about quality, especially evident on the website of the State Board for Educator Certification (SBEC) and other materials, can be amusing.

For example, Texas's 2008 Title II Report states that because the state only admits candidates holding bachelor's degrees into alternative certification programs, these individuals "possess a strong foundation of content knowledge prior to entering the classroom" (U.S. Department of Education 2009c). Right.

In Texas, the toughest alternative programs require only twenty-one hours of course work in the subject area, zero hours of courses in pedagogy, and zero field experience. Although the SBEC claims that alternative certification programs offer "comprehensive pre-service training" (State Board for Educator Certification 2009), in most programs there is no pre-service training at all. Similarly, the SBEC calls the first year of teaching "practice teaching," though parents might not be impressed that the alternatively certified teacher's first experience with children often coincides with his or her first day on the job.

The fact that Texas does not have an initial or probationary certification helps keep everything muddled. All candidates in Texas, irrespective of their education or experience, receive the same certificate. Furthermore, once an individual receives a certificate, there is no room for improvement. The initial certificate is the one and only level in the Texas system. The state provides no pay increments for an MA, a PhD, or national-board certification.

During 2005–2006 in Texas, 36,114 teachers were certified through universities or colleges (half of these were enrolled in alternative programs run by universities); and 16,638 teachers were alternatively certified by for-profit businesses, educational service centers, community colleges, or school districts (Texas Public Education Information Resource 2007). In other words, 34,000 of Texas's teachers, or 68 percent (!), were alternatively certified in 2005–2006, while traditional, university-based certification programs provided the state with only 32 percent of its teachers.

Part of the reason for the transmogrification of teacher certification in Texas was the gold-rush mentality of entrepreneurs who flooded the state with programs in the hope of striking it rich once teacher certification was freed from university control. However, as with the California Gold Rush of the 1850s and the Klondike Gold Rush of the 1890s, the Texas Certification Gold Rush of today has left many speculators bankrupt. In 2007 alone, twenty-three of Texas's alternative licensure programs closed or filed for bankruptcy.

More than seventy alternative programs in Texas survive, and they range from totally online courses to programs requiring at least a few face-to-face interactions. One of the largest alternative programs is iteach-TEXAS, which offers all courses online. IteachTEXAS emphasizes the following advantages on its website, which places it firmly in the Level I: Cram classification:

- Upon acceptance, immediate enrollment in instructional course work
- No arbitrary deadline for enrollment
- Instruction on candidate's time schedule
- No required on-site meetings
- Customized instructional work
- Program study guides available in many content areas (iteachTEXAS 2009)

According to the iteachTEXAS website, the curriculum is self-paced, involving an introductory course (Overview of The Road to Certification) and "six instructional courses . . . designed to be completed within a six-month time span" (iteachTEXAS 2009). Because rigor is important, candidates are not allowed to progress faster than one course every ten days. *One course every ten days.* Most assignments are "computer-graded."

Requirements for admission to iteachTEXAS:

- A 2.5 grade point average overall, or 2.5 in the last sixty course hours, or 2.5 in content courses
- Demonstrated basic competence in reading, writing, and math*
- Eighteen hours of content (to teach grades 4–8), or twenty-one hours of content (to teach grades 8–12)

* A combined score of 700 on the Graduate Record Exam (GRE) verbal and GRE quantitative tests would satisfy this requirement, although such a score would place the individual among the lowest 10 percent of test-takers.

IteachTEXAS candidates get a job right away, then complete a one-year mentoring process, as dictated by the state. According to iteach-TEXAS (2009),

> Once a candidate is hired by a district, the candidate is enrolled in EDTC5700—You're Hired. This course provides detailed information for the newly hired teacher. All hired candidates are required to submit self-reflections and classroom reflections during their field experience.

In the case of iteachTEXAS, field experience = the candidate's first year as a fully paid teacher.

If the plethora of alternative certification programs is not enough, candidates can also begin teaching in Texas through a temporary teacher certification (TTC) without having to go to the trouble of iteachTEXAS. According to the State Board for Educator Certification (2009),

> TTC provides an additional certification route for persons who hold a bachelor's degree . . . to enter the teaching profession.
>
> Persons requesting a TTC must be employed by a Texas school district for the two-year validity period of the certificate. The school district will assume the responsibility of training.

Obviously, Texas considers Level I: Cram inadequate preparation for the teachers of its children, so it also offers Level 0: Zilch as a second option.

While iteachTEXAS, the second-largest alternative provider in the state, produces 1,500–2,000 new teachers per year, the graduating class of teachers at the University of Texas at Austin rarely exceeds 150 students.

Of course, the University of Texas at Austin has stringent admission criteria and offers only one path through its program: a lengthy and demanding combination of courses in pedagogy and field experience. On the other hand, iteachTEXAS requires only a few Internet courses taken at the student's convenience, no field hours, and no student teaching. Table 2.5 compares the two programs, both of which lead to the same certification.

Level I: Cram, Example 2: The ABCTE in Pennsylvania

Pennsylvania subcontracts alternative certification to the ABCTE (Pennsylvania Department of Education 2009). As in New Hampshire and all states in which the ABCTE is accepted as legitimate, ABCTE customers in Pennsylvania do not have to bother with PRAXIS I or PRAXIS II. Instead, they take a computer-based exam created by the ABCTE and assessed by the ABCTE at an ABCTE regional center. The ABCTE's "professional teaching knowledge" multiple-choice test requires that candidates get 54 percent of the answers correct. The content-area exams require between 50 percent (general science) and 61 percent (reading) correct answers.

However, unlike the ABCTE in other states, the ABCTE in Pennsylvania requires a modicum of additional preparation. ABCTE customers in Pennsylvania must log a total of ten days of face-to-face interactions. Requirements include the following:

1. Attendance at two one-day retreats
2. Completion of two four-day graduate-level courses offered through St. Joseph's University Learning Institute (see below)

This moves the ABCTE in Pennsylvania from Level 0: Zilch into the category of Level I: Cram.

The ABCTE-approved course offerings for fall 2008 at St. Joseph's University Learning Institute (2008) included a course on violence in the media taught by a former police officer with a master's degree in criminal justice, and Diversity: Creating a Caring Community, taught by the coach of a girls' local lacrosse team.

Fall 2008 costs for ABCTE programs, which included ABCTE tests in pedagogy and the subject area, ranged from $395 (reading) to $975

Table 2.5. Comparison of IteachTEXAS (Level I: Cram) with Traditional Programs at the University of Texas at Austin

Name	Minimum GPA	Average ACT/ SAT	Hours in Content	Hours in Education	Hours in Methods of Teaching Content	Pre-Student-Teaching Field Experience	Student Teaching	Other Distinguishing Features
IteachTEXAS	2.5 in content or overall (last 60 hours)	None	18	6 online courses	0	None	None	Delivered online in its entirety in six months; 350 on the GRE Verbal waives basic-skills test requirement
University of Texas at Austin, English Education	2.75	23/1120	36, plus 12 in a minor	31	10	Extensive	Full semester, full time	Postbaccalaureate collaboration with the College of Liberal Arts; 3-semester program; besides field experience, there is a practicum component of several other courses; certified in grades 8–12; induction support for graduates and novice teachers, including online mentoring by experienced, currently practicing teachers

(continued)

Table 2.5. (*continued*)

Name	Minimum GPA	Average ACT/ SAT	Hours in Content	Hours in Education	Hours in Methods of Teaching Content	Pre-Student-Teaching Field Experience	Student Teaching	Other Distinguishing Features
University of Texas at Austin, Math Education	2.50	SAT II Math 501–800	32	18	5	Extensive full time	Full semester,	Postbaccalaureate collaboration with the College of Liberal Arts; 3-semester program; besides field experience, there is a practicum component of several other courses; certified in grades 8–12; induction support for graduates and novice teachers, including online mentoring by experienced, currently practicing teachers

(special education), plus a mentoring fee of $800, plus the cost of preparation materials (up to $600), plus the student's choice of two courses at the Learning Institute ($780 each, or $1,560 plus the cost of accommodations and meals). Candidates who go through the ABCTE receive Pennsylvania's Professional Instructional I Certificate by the end of the first year. Again, in the eight other states where the ABCTE is approved, students are not required to take courses.

Pennsylvania State University's teacher-preparation program, notable for its high admissions standards, provides a stark contrast to the ABCTE program. In addition to a 3.0 grade point requirement for entry, the average Penn State student has an ACT score of 26 and must pass an additional exam relating to special education before being recommended for licensure. (See table 2.6.)

While ABCTE students are taking courses such as Diversity: Creating a Caring Community, taught by the coach of a girls' local lacrosse team, Penn State students are loading up on years' worth of courses in content, education, and methods of teaching taught by PhD-holding experts, and are accumulating field hours.

Level I: Cram, Example 3: Alternative certification through selected institutions of higher education in Kansas

Kansas runs alternative certification through these institutions of higher education: Baker, Emporia State, Fort Hays State, MidAmerica Nazarene, Newman, Ottawa, Pittsburg State, Southwestern, the University of Kansas, the University of St. Mary, Washburn, and Wichita State. Candidates seeking a restricted teaching license begin teaching immediately and take course work while they work and during summers.

The alternative program at Fort Hays State University, Transition to Teaching, produced about as many teachers as did Fort Hays's traditional programs in 2008, and the program is growing rapidly. However, the differences are vast between programs for alternatively certified candidates seeking a restricted license at Fort Hays and candidates pursuing a five-year program at the University of Kansas.

Candidates at Fort Hays take on the full-time duties of a teacher via a restricted license after participating in a four-day (!) orientation. Over the course of a year, they complete twenty hours of online course work.

Table 2.6. Comparison of the ABCTE (Level I: Cram) in Pennsylvania with Traditional Programs at Pennsylvania State University

Name	Minimum GPA	Hours in Content	Hours in Education	Hours in Methods of Teaching Content	Pre-Student-Teaching Field Experience	Student Teaching	Other Distinguishing Features
ABCTE	None	0	10 days training	0	None	None	ABCTE customers do not have to take PRAXIS II.
Pennsylvania State University, English Education	3.0	63	42	32	Yes	Full time, full semester	Requires Pre-Certification Competency Exam on Educating Students with Disabilities
Pennsylvania State University, Math Education	3.0	63	42	32	Yes	Full time, full semester	Requires Pre-Certification Competency Exam on Educating Students with Disabilities

According to the *Licensed Personnel Report State Profile 2007–2008* (Kansas State Department of Education Teacher Education and Licensure, and B. Fultz 2008), of the 1,401 new teachers certified in Kansas, 309 (22 percent) were certified in this manner through a restricted teaching license.

Candidates in the Transition to Teaching program at Fort Hays only need to have twenty-one hours of subject area course work, take PRAXIS II at the end of the first year, and take PRAXIS PLT (Principles of Learning and Teaching) at the end of year three. While candidates at the University of Kansas are shelling out thousands of dollars for a slate of graduate-level courses and twenty weeks' worth of field experience in a final year of preparation, candidates at Fort Hays are receiving full-time pay while pointing and clicking from home. (See table 2.7.)

Level II: Minimal

Explanation: Minimal course work and minimal field experience before full-time teaching.

Examples:

1. The New Jersey Alternative Program at the Liberty Science Center
2. Alternative Routes to Certification (ARTC) in Delaware
3. Kaplan University in Iowa

Similar programs: One-size-fits-all alternative programs at state universities, community colleges, and businesses

Level II: Minimal, Example 1: The New Jersey Alternative Program at the Liberty Science Center

Candidates who hold a bachelor's degree and want to teach are welcome in New Jersey. Little preparation is needed. There is no incentive to go the route of Teach For America, which at least provides a support structure and a few weeks of seminars before the first day of class. New Jersey requires nothing for a teaching license but a contract and a positive recommendation at the end of the year from the school principal.

Table 2.7. Comparison of the Transition to Teaching Program (Level I: Cram) at Fort Hays State University with Traditional Programs at the University of Kansas

Name	Minimum GPA	Total Hours	Hours in Content	Hours in Education	Hours in Methods of Teaching Content	Pre-Student-Teaching Field Experiences	Student Teaching	Other Distinguishing Features
Fort Hays State University, Transition to Teaching Program	2.5	26 (all online)	Students may begin with as few as 21 hours in the content area	20	0	None (students are given 6 hours of credit for the job of full-time teacher)	None	Four-day orientation is the only time students meet face to face with faculty; neither PRAXIS II nor PRAXIS PLT is required for a teaching position

Program								
University of Kansas, English Education	2.75	124	30	48	12	More than 8 weeks	12-week, full-time internship	Five-year undergraduate program includes full-year field experience; candidates must pass PRAXIS II and PRAXIS PLT before receiving initial license
University of Kansas, Mathematics Education	2.75	128–137	42–44	48	6	More than 8 weeks	12-week, full-time internship	Five-year undergraduate program includes full-year field experience; candidates must pass PRAXIS II and PRAXIS PLT before receiving initial license

New Jersey considers teacher-certification programs at community colleges to be traditional teacher preparation, so community college–based programs will not be considered here (see chapter 3).

In New Jersey, even a science museum can license teachers. On the website of the Liberty Science Center, alongside admission prices, hours of operation, and facility rental information, one can find information on teacher licensure. According to the website, "Participants complete most of their training in an intensive 20-day summer program at the Science Center and observe and teach lessons in a local summer school program before they begin their first teaching positions" (Liberty Science Center 2009). One assumes that candidates for alternative certification also receive discounts on admission tickets to the museum.

The rigor of the five-year program in teacher preparation at Rutgers University with its over 150 hours of preparation; three field experiences prior to full-time, full-semester student teaching; high average SAT; a portfolio submission; and other requirements is in stark relief to the relaxed standards of the alternative program at the Liberty Science Center. According to the New Jersey Department of Education (2009a), "By allowing the completion of formal instruction in the essential pedagogy necessary for success in the classroom, in conjunction with supervised employment, the program has redefined eligibility."

Indeed, eligibility for teacher certification in New Jersey, an early adopter of alternative certification programs, continues to get redefined. No wonder that, in recent years, alternative programs have experienced tremendous growth while enrollments in teacher-preparation programs at Rutgers have declined.

New Jersey's 2007 Title II Report (U.S. Department of Education 2009c) is full of contradictions, grammatical errors, and incorrect information. For example, in the report it is stated that the Certificate of Eligibility (CE) and the Certificate of Eligibility with Advanced Standing (CEAS) are lifetime certificates, although they are only temporary, two-year certificates. The 2007 Title II Report also states that there are no requirements for license renewal, only to note a few pages later that "to maintain the standard certificate, the teacher must complete a minimum of 100 hours of approved professional development every five years." (See table 2.8.)

Table 2.8. Comparison of the Alternative Certification Program (Level II: Minimal) at Liberty Science Center with Traditional Programs at Rutgers University Main Campus

Name	Minimum GPA	Mean SAT	Total Prepparation Time	Hours in Content	Prepparation Time	Hours in Methods of Teaching Content	Pre-student-Teaching experience	Student Teaching	Other Distinguishing Features
Liberty Science Center, New Jersey Alternative Certification Program	None	None	20 days	30-hour minimum; only 3 hours (one course) required at the 4000 level	20 days	0	Possibly some tutoring at the Science Center during the summer	None	Discounts on admission to the museum
Rutgers University, English Education	2.8	1160	5 years, 150+ hours (120 undergraduate and 30+ in a fifth year)	30	10 courses, or 30 hours over several years	15	Yes	Full time, full semester	Students complete a baccalaureate degree in English and move into a fifth year of study
Rutgers University, Math Education	2.8	1160	5 years, 150+ hours (120 undergraduate and 30+ in a fifth year)	45	10 courses, or 30 hours over several years	20	Yes	Full time, full semester	Students complete a baccalaureate degree in math and move into a fifth year of study

*Level II: Minimal, Example 2: Alternative Routes to
Certification (ARTC) in Delaware*

According to a recent report,

> ARTC teachers are now at least 10 percent of all Delaware teachers of Eng-
> lish, mathematics, Spanish, French, and German; 20 percent to 25 percent
> of all teachers of biology, chemistry, physical science, earth science and
> technology education; one-third of all teachers of business and Latin; and
> almost half of all teachers of physics (Hughes 2007).

ARTC is a one-year program in which candidates take fifteen hours of
courses and go through a first-year mentorship program required of all
new Delaware teachers.

Requirements for the ARTC program:

- Passing score on Praxis I assessments in reading, writing, and mathematics
- Job offer
- Fifteen credit hours of graduate-level, professional-education course
  work (includes effective teaching strategies, adolescent development,
  classroom management, teaching methods in the content area, introduc-
  tion to secondary special-education, reading in the content area, and
  multicultural education)*
- Successful completion of a new-teacher induction program (involves
  three visits during the year)

*Ideally, candidates begin the program in the summer before they enter
the classroom, but "late hires" may also begin the program in the fall
or spring. Two to three courses meet in the summer, in all-day, two-to-
three-week sessions. Courses during the school year meet on occasional
Saturdays.

Praxis II in the content area is not required to participate in ARTC.
However, the candidate must pass Praxis II PLT in order to qualify for a
continuing license.

One alternative program in Delaware, the Alternative Route to Teacher
Education (ARTE) is run through the University of Delaware. Candidates

who pass PRAXIS I can begin teaching right away, though they must take fifteen "fast-track" graduate courses (as in two-week courses over the summer) through the University of Delaware.

Although the legislation that authorized ARTC stipulated that candidates must have completed 120 clock hours in a modified field experience, the requirement is often waived for candidates who decide late that they want a full-time job (despite their lack of preparation and experience). In many subject areas, half or more of new hires (Hughes 2007) are alternatively certified.

Vast differences exist between the requirements for teaching certification in the traditional program at the University of Delaware and those available through ARTC. Students at the University of Delaware have an average SAT score of 1184, take thirty-nine to forty-one hours in content and thirteen hours in specialized teaching methods, have numerous pre-student-teaching experiences, and student teach for a full semester, while students in ARTC take education courses in two-week sessions over the summer and avoid field experience. (See table 2.9.)

Level II: Minimal, Example 3: Kaplan University in Iowa

At the beginning of 2008–2009 the Iowa Department of Education reported declining enrollments in 69 percent of Iowa's schools. Yet in February 2007, Kaplan University was granted permission by the legislature to offer online, alternative certification programs at the postbaccalaureate and master's levels.

According to a press release from Kaplan University (2007), these programs were launched "to address Iowa's critical teacher shortage." With declining enrollments across the state, perhaps it is also possible that, because Kaplan's corporate office is located in Davenport, Iowa, it may enjoy favorite-son status with state legislators.

Kaplan's alternative program is called the Teacher Intern Program, and it has two requirements:

- Bachelor's degree with a grade point average of 2.5
- Three years of work experience

Table 2.9. Comparison of the Alternative Route to Teacher Certification (ARTC; Level II: Minimal) in Delaware with Traditional Programs at the University of Delaware

Name	Average SAT	Hours in Content	Hours in Education	Hours in Methods of Teaching Content	Pre-Student-Teaching Field Experience	Student Teaching	Other Distinguishing Features
ARTC in math or in English	None; Praxis I basic-skills test	30-hour minimum	15	0	Possibly limited tutoring or field experience the summer before employment	None	Program provides more than half of new teachers in many subject areas.
University of Delaware, English Education	1184	39	29	13	Extensive and varied	Full time, full semester	Field experience over several semesters
University of Delaware, Mathematics Education	1184	41	21	8	Extensive and varied	Full time, full semester	Field experience for 3 years

Kaplan's Teacher Intern Program consists of the following parts:

- Twelve semester hours of introductory content completed prior to the beginning of the academic year that includes (1) learning environment/ classroom management; (2) instructional planning; (3) instructional strategies; (4) student learning; (5) diverse learners; (6) collaboration, ethics, and relationships; (7) assessment; and (8) fifty contact hours in the field prior to the candidate's initial employment
- Four semester hours of a teacher-intern seminar during the teacher-internship year to include support and extension of course work from the teacher-intern introductory content
- Twelve semester hours of content including (1) foundations, reflection, and professional development; (2) communication; (3) exceptional learners; (4) reading strategies; and (5) computer technology

Although fifty "contact hours in the field" prior to the candidate's employment may seem insufficient, especially when compared to the field hours required in traditional programs, it is nevertheless fifty more hours than is offered by Level 0: Zilch and Level 1: Cram programs. (See table 2.10.)

Level III: Adequate

Explanation: Course work with several different kinds of field experience, including student teaching

Example: The University of Oregon

Similar programs: Alternative certification programs at large research universities that use the same requirements for entry, performance, and exit for both traditional and nontraditional students

Level III: Adequate, Example 1: The University of Oregon

Oregon has an impressive system for teacher preparation that requires the same level of performance of all teachers, even those hired on temporary, emergency certificates. Teachers hired in emergency shortage situations receive a restricted transitional teaching license, and are not considered highly qualified. Part of the credit for Oregon's caring approach must go

Table 2.10. Comparison of Kaplan University's Teacher Intern Program (Level II: Minimal) with Traditional Programs at the University of Iowa

Name	Minimum GPA	Average ACT/SAT	Hours in Content	Hours in Education	Hours in Methods of Teaching Content	Pre-Student-Teaching Field Experience	Student Teaching	Other Distinguishing Features
Kaplan University, Teacher Intern Program	2.5 (state requirement)	None	0	29	0	Some (arranged through Kaplan)	None	All courses delivered online
University of Iowa, English Education	2.7	23/1080	33	24	18	Yes	14 weeks, full time	Dual degree in English and education
University of Iowa, Mathematics Education	2.7	23/1080	37	27	12	Yes	14 weeks, full time	Dual degree in math and education

to the Teacher Standards and Practices Commission, whose membership includes teachers, administrators, school-board members, and parents. Such a partnership among these diverse constituents assures citizens of the state that teacher certification in Oregon still has meaning.

Oregon is singular in its honesty—it is the only state in the union that openly recognizes that individuals with temporary licenses do not meet the definition of *highly qualified teacher* under the federal No Child Left Behind Act. The alternative certification program at the University of Oregon is, per se, not alternative, because it cuts no corners and holds all students to the same levels of performance.

However, the program is expressly designed for students who have already graduated with a bachelor's degree in the subject area. Entry to the University of Oregon's master's level, teacher-preparation programs requires a bachelor's degree in the subject area, a 3.0 grade point average, and preparation in both special education and Teaching English to Speakers of Other Languages (TESOL).

The mean SAT score for University of Oregon students is 1100. The University of Oregon's program is field-intensive, with numerous campus courses offering opportunities to work in the local schools. In many ways, programs such as those at the University of Oregon (see table 2.11) share similarities with preparation programs in high-achieving countries such as Finland and Singapore (see chapter 4).

THE ADEQUACY OF ALTERNATIVE CERTIFICATION

What constitutes adequate preparation for a teacher? Standards for the preparation of teachers have been developed by the National Council for the Accreditation of Teacher Education (NCATE). According to NCATE, the only alternative programs in the United States that are of acceptable quality are based in universities and colleges.

That is, every alternative teacher-certification program operating out of a business, school district, or regional service center in the country fails to meet the minimum standards of adequacy as defined by NCATE. These alternative programs fail to address most, if not all, of the following areas:

1. Content knowledge and ability to teach in the subject area (standard 1)
2. Disposition suitable for a career as a teacher (standard 1)

Table 2.11. Alternative Teacher-Certification Programs at the University of Oregon

Name	Minimum GPA	Average SAT	Total Hours	Hours in Content (Includes Undergraduate)	Hours in Education (Graduate)	Hours in Methods of Teaching Content (Graduate)	Pre-Student-Teaching Field Experience (Graduate)	Student Teaching (Graduate)	Other Distinguishing Features
University of Oregon, English Education	3.0	1100	Bachelor's degree plus master's courses (up to 50 hours)	29	50	11	Yes	Full semester, as required by law	Five-year program leading to bachelor's degree in English, licensure, and possible master's in education
University of Oregon, Math Education	3.0	1100	Bachelor's degree plus master's courses (up to 50 hours)	28	50	11	Yes	Full semester, as required by law	Five-year program leading to bachelor's degree in Math, licensure, and possible master's in education

Note: The hour totals have been converted from quarter hours to semester hours.

3. Appropriate field experiences prior to teaching (standard 2)
4. Supervision in early teaching experiences (standard 2)
5. Awareness of diversity (standard 3)
6. Ability to work in a variety of school settings (standard 3)
7. Credentials of faculty delivering the program (standard 5)

Examples of alternative programs operating at the Level 0: Zilch, Level I: Cram, and Level II: Minimal levels abound. Operating alongside these quick-and-easy programs are university-based alternative programs, which are neither quick nor easy. However, the fact that a preparation program is university-based is no assurance of quality.

Many universities have scrambled to benefit from the certification gold rush by creating non-NCATE-approved alternative programs that run side by side with their NCATE-approved programs. Unfortunately, of the 1,400 or so institutions that prepare teachers, many are ineffective and inefficient, and seem content to remain that way.

Chapter Three

The Walmart Effect and University-Based Teacher Preparation

A look at the history of teacher preparation reveals a tension between two fundamental approaches:

1. Attracting academically accomplished individuals to the profession
2. Educating whoever wants to teach to become a teacher

New suppliers of teachers such as Teach For America are, in actuality, not preparation programs at all. Rather their focus is on *attracting academically accomplished individuals to the profession*, at least for a few years. The totality of the preparation program for Teach For America students is paltry and brief—usually five weeks of classroom instruction—followed by full-time teaching and the hope of strong mentorship by a seasoned professional.

From the 1960s to the 1980s, when preparation for the teaching profession was almost exclusively the domain of universities and colleges, the focus was on *educating whoever wants to teach to become a teacher* with an emphasis on taking "whoever walked through the door." However, with the surge of alternative certification, many universities now educate fewer teachers than do businesses, school districts, and governmental agencies.

While alternative certification has proliferated, agencies such as the National Council for Accreditation of Teacher Education (NCATE) have increased requirements for accreditation. These contradictory trends—the loosening of requirements through alternative certification and the tightening of standards by accreditation agencies—have caused teacher preparation at universities and colleges to change in surprising ways.

Tired of losing students to quick-and-easy alternative programs, some universities have responded by joining the gold rush for certification dollars by developing profitable, separate, off-site programs. For example, the University of North Texas offers a relatively small, NCATE-accredited certification program on its campus in Denton, Texas, but it also offers an Internet-based, non-NCATE-accredited, twelve-hour certification program that competes with the multitude of quick-and-easy programs in Texas, such as iteachTEXAS and Teach For America. The University of North Texas (2009) describes its program as follows:

> The Online Teacher Certification Program was designed for mature students who have a bachelor's degree and want to earn initial secondary teacher certification at the graduate level. The program consists of 12 graduate credit hours and a 6 hour mentored internship. Content for all four courses is delivered 100% online.

As with most such programs, field experience in the Online Teacher Certification Program at North Texas is negligible or nonexistent. If a student is already working in a school, all field requirements are waived.

Institutions like the University of North Texas, formerly known as "normal schools," whose historical focus has been teacher preparation, routinely produce the largest numbers of teachers within a state. In fact, the enrollments of prospective teachers at the largest teacher-education-focused institutions, sometimes referred to pejoratively as "teacher factories," dwarf the number of teachers being trained at other institutions.

For example, while the University of North Texas enrolls prospective teachers by the thousands; the largest university in the state, the University of Texas at Austin, graduated only 142 students in 2007–2008.

Certainly one of the difficulties with the decentralization of certification has been keeping track of the number of freshly certified teachers from new vendors. In California, in addition to the growing list of alternative providers, over eighty organizations now claim university status and have the state's blessing to prepare teachers. Some institutions, such as Chapman University, may have a physical campus somewhere in California with trees, buildings, sidewalks, and libraries, but many universities that train new teachers are "campuses without walls."

For example, the majority of Chapman's students never set foot on an actual campus, and they complete requirements over the Internet. Programs taken through Chapman or the University of Phoenix, a national franchise of online graduate-education that has set up sales offices in cities nationwide, are no longer considered alternative in California or in many other states. Instead, these programs are considered both traditional and university-based.

Like Chapman, National University has a small, accredited under-graduate program on a physical campus in California, but it makes most of its money through a massive, non-NCATE-accredited graduate program offered online. As with Chapman and Phoenix, National offers both teacher certification and a master's degree in a single package. Ac-cording to National University's promotional materials, field experience and student teaching may be waived for prospective students who spent time at "summer school, after school programs, and outdoor education programs."

How large are these programs in comparison to other teacher-education programs? In California in 2007–2008, the University of Phoenix's tra-ditional program certified 511 new teachers as well as 41 students in an alternative program; Chapman University certified 478 in traditional programs and 347 in an alternative program; and National University certified 1,382 students through its traditional program and another 532 teachers through its alternative program. Thus the three programs certi-fied 3,300 or so new teachers in California in 2007–2008, or more than twenty-seven times the total of new teachers (115) who graduated from the University of Southern California (USC) during the same time period.

In response to the onslaught of quick-and-easy certification offered by its new competitors, USC altered its teacher-preparation programs so that only one option is now available to all prospective teachers: a master of arts in teaching program compressed into a uniform, thirteen-month block of courses and field experiences. Recently, USC has started an aggressive advertising campaign for an online version of the already shortened pro-gram, compressed even further into twelve months, and available online nationwide.

USC is representative of how university-based teacher preparation is starting to evolve (or devolve) around the country. The transformation of teacher preparation from an altruistic endeavor established for the public good and run by universities to a profit-focused business enterprise run by corporations is fundamentally changing the way teachers are taught.

As Walmart has proven again and again in retail sales, in a competitive business environment, the organization able to offer products at the lowest-possible price point wins. In order to survive, universities have been forced to reconceptualize teacher-preparation programs in new ways that minimize costs so that their programs can be competitively priced against corporate providers.

Cost-cutting has led to streamlining programs, eliminating electives, and cutting any courses that do not adhere to acceptable levels of profit. Across the country, the most expensive courses, i.e., those that are most personnel-intensive and require seminars, mentored field experiences, faculty-supervised projects, and master's theses, are disappearing.

In point of fact, USC's new online master's program offers no seminars, no faculty-supervised field experiences, and no thesis. Instead, the program is comprised of a slate of generic courses with a standardized electronic portfolio tacked on at the end.

The emergence of USC's highly promoted, low-cost, Internet-based master's program is only one of the first of what promises to be an avalanche of such new-age, university-based, teacher-preparation programs to come. The Walmart effect, which compelled USC to change its philosophy toward teacher preparation, has helped propel the ascendancy of formerly alternative programs run by corporations such as the University of Phoenix, Grand Canyon University, Kaplan, ad infinitum, to equal stature with long-established universities.

Indeed, as a perusal of state department of education websites confirms, Internet-based, formerly alternative programs are often promoted with great fanfare over on-campus degrees at state universities. As a result, these corporate-run programs continue to grow ever-larger enrollments.

However, not all colleges of education are getting faster and cheaper. Instead of succumbing to the lure of a fast buck, a few institutions have ramped up admissions standards and program requirements, mandating lengthy graduate experiences replete with one- or two-year internships.

One example of an institution that has taken a step forward rather than a step back is Neag College of Education at the University of Connecticut (UConn). While Teach For America in Connecticut requires only five weeks of preparation, UConn requires five years. In fact, UConn also requires field experiences spread over six semesters of progressively more challenging work. Every UConn student participates in at least one placement in an urban setting, one placement in a special-education setting, and one K–12 experience. Still more field work is expected in a post-student-teaching internship.

The College of Education at Michigan State University is another institution that has grown stronger rather than weaker in response to the rapid commercialization of teacher preparation. Students at Michigan State pursue a major in the content area (usually around forty hours), take fifty hours in education courses (including twelve hours of content-specific course work), and engage in two field experiences before taking on a year-long internship in the schools.

Some colleges of education located within research institutions (formerly called *research institutions,* now called *research extensive institutions*) have started posting notices on their websites and promotional materials explicitly stating, "We are offering no alternative programs at this time" to notify students seeking no-sweat routes to certification that they are not available. The postings have become a necessity as more and more institutions are responding to the struggle to find ways to remain economically viable by creating high-profit, low-cost programs.

Recently, some universities have even begun swimming in the dangerous waters of subcontracting. That is, some universities have begun contracting with corporations to deliver their programs in teacher education. Subcontracting is popular in computer technology, where a call to a help line concerning a new laptop has a better chance of landing in India than Indiana. But up to now, subcontracting in universities has not gained many adherents. One assumed that a degree from a university meant that the student learned from faculty at that university. No more.

Today, some future teachers are being taught and assessed by poorly paid, part-time workers hired by a corporation. This has happened most famously at Lamar University in Beaumont, Texas. The College of Education at Lamar was struggling to maintain enrollments, and the reputation of its teachers was not stellar. So Lamar decided to subcontract its programs to a corporation, Higher Ed Holdings (HEH), that offered increases in enrollment via distance education in exchange for control over the university's programs in teacher education.

As per the demands of HEH, all master's degrees were redesigned to fit into five-week modules that could be delivered online. The new, online master's degree at Lamar is a one-size-fits-all model that can be delivered to one thousand customers simultaneously. Money is paid up front by students, but tuition is at a significant discount to the university's on-campus offerings. Tests and papers are graded by computer and by part-time staff hired by HEH.

In institutions such as Michigan State University and the University of Connecticut, rigorous course work, high grade point requirements, and numerous field experiences serve as multiple checkpoints to weed out weaker, less-determined teachers. The problem of poor teacher quality is nonexistent in such programs.

The quick-and-easy, university-based programs that have been created to compete with cheap, corporate programs commonly have no checkpoints and few requirements because they are competing on cost, not quality. The HEH program at Lamar University has few checkpoints, requires no field experience, and offers no chance at seminars or theses. Instead, HEH offers convenience and speed—an entire master's program can be completed during leisure hours, sitting at home, in less than six months.

COMMUNITY COLLEGES AS
CENTERS FOR GRADUATE EDUCATION

Community colleges, once the institutions of choice for high-school students who wanted to spend their freshman year of college near home, have suddenly been given the green light to offer postbaccalaureate degrees in education, and the right to recommend teachers for certification in several states: New Jersey, Texas, Mississippi, Arizona, and New Mexico.

As in most states, community colleges in Arizona are forbidden from offering courses at the junior or senior levels, but they are free to offer graduate courses in education. Typically, community-college, teacher-preparation programs are offered online in "accelerated formats," with a few field experiences thrown in along with the promise of "master teacher" supervision during student teaching. As in New Jersey, programs offered through community colleges in Arizona are considered mainline, state-board-approved programs; they are not considered alternative certification programs.

In New Mexico, teacher preparation at the community college is considered alternative, though a movement in the state appears underway to relocate all teacher-preparation programs from universities to community colleges. Teacher-preparation programs at community colleges in New Mexico, like the one at Santa Fe Community College, involve eighteen hours of course work—all delivered online. However, Santa Fe Community College, like most New Mexico community colleges, requires field experience, though brief and limited.

The worst community-college-based teacher-preparation program in the nation may be in Mississippi. The Mississippi Alternate Path to Quality Teachers (MAPQT) requires only a C average (2.0 GPA) for admission, ninety clock hours of seminars (held online and through community colleges), and a passing score on the PRAXIS I basic-skills test. Like customers of the ABCTE (which Mississippi has also embraced), MAPQT students are exempt from passing the PRAXIS II content exam.

For the 2005–2006 year, almost three hundred Mississippians enrolled in MAPQT (Section 37-3-2 Nontraditional Teacher Preparation Internship Programs 2009), and the program continues to grow. Popular MAPQT certification areas for 2005–2006 included English (forty-eight students), social studies (thirty-seven students), and physical education (twenty-four students). Less-popular certification areas were chemistry (one student) and physics (zero students).

MAPQT students do not have to bother with field experience, student teaching, knowledge of content, or subject-specific methods courses. Nor are they required to furnish evidence of mastery of pedagogy at any point in their program.

These are the new breed of teachers that Mississippi is hiring: individuals with a 2.0 grade point average who managed to remain conscious for ninety clock hours of Internet surfing. Somehow, the prospect that this new breed of untrained teachers will lead Mississippi out of its place as fiftieth-ranked state in terms of student achievement seems improbable.

UNDERMINING UNIVERSITY-BASED TEACHER PREPARATION THROUGH STATE POLICY-MAKING

In his "2009 State of Education" speech, Arizona state superintendent Tom Horne extolled his achievements in the preparation of teachers, which included bringing a market-based approach to certification.

Under my administration, we have broken the monopoly that limited the supply of teachers to those going through conventional teaching programs. We have supported Teach For America program which has been flourishing in Arizona. We began an Alternative Pathways program under which those with substantive Bachelor's Degrees, who passed a subject matter test, could begin teaching after a six week summer program in teaching methods (Horne 2009).

The unnamed holder of the monopoly on certification in Horne's speech is the university system. What is incredible about Horne's speech is that he is not a governor ruled by party dictates or a senator with a personal vendetta; he is *the state superintendent of education.*

Horne is precisely the kind of powerful official that one would expect to be in favor of well-educated teachers, but he is not. Instead, Horne is in favor of abundant and cheap teachers. To make teachers abundant and cheap in Arizona, he gave businesses, community colleges, school districts, and the Arizona Department of Education the right to certify.

Like Horne, political representatives across the nation have opted for quantity over quality with regard to teachers. A law passed during Florida governor Jeb Bush's tenure required all school districts to devise alternative teacher-preparation programs that could be operated without the "impediments" of universities or accrediting agencies.

According to the website of the Florida Department of Education (2009b), "Each Florida school district must offer a competency-based, on-the-job alternative certification program—either a district-developed program that has been approved by the Florida Department of Education or the Florida Alternative Certification Program." There may be 32 universities and colleges that prepare teachers in Florida, but there are 111 other agencies, such as community colleges, K–12 schools, or counties, that may prepare teachers as well.

Recently, laws governing teacher certification in Indiana were altered so that every institution of higher education had to offer a Transition to Teaching (TTT) program. According to the Indiana Department of Education website, "Transition to Teaching is based on the premise that the candidate already has the content knowledge in the licensing area" (Indiana Department of Education 2009).

The TTT program consists of eighteen hours of course work for secondary applicants and twenty-four hours of course work for elementary applicants. Universities were forced to participate in TTT by the state legislature, even if they considered the program a sham.

THE SUBTEXT OF NEW MENTORING LEGISLATION

In several states, worries over large numbers of inexperienced, alternatively certified teachers have resulted in new legislation mandating close mentoring during the first year of teaching. For example, West Virginia has an elaborate beginning-teacher program that requires a team of a school principal, a member of the county professional-staff-development council, and an experienced classroom teacher to serve as a committee to oversee a new teacher's development.

The experienced classroom teacher is supposed to log at least one hour per week in observations for the first half of the year and one hour every two weeks for the second half. The mentor is also supposed to meet with the candidate at least once per week throughout the year and to plan monthly evaluation sessions focusing upon the first-year teacher's development. For this time-intensive work, the mentor only receives six hundred dollars.

In this way, mentorship programs have become more common in PK–12 schools, but for the wrong reasons. Instead of serving as a useful strategy for matching rookie teachers with seasoned master teachers, mentoring has become the sole way for many new teachers to learn how to teach.

Obviously, a new teacher who walks into a school after a couple weeks of training in the MAPQT way will require more help than the new teacher who graduates from the University of Connecticut's five-year program with its six semesters of carefully choreographed field experience and a year-long internship. States have figured out that it is the mentor who must make up the difference. A great mentor can accomplish much, but there is the small difficulty of the mentor's responsibilities to his or her own students while mentoring.

Thus, while mentoring has always been heralded as a crucial checkpoint for new teachers, the kind of mentoring required to transform neophytes with no academic preparation and no practical experience into real teachers would be a challenge for anyone, let alone someone who already has a full-time job and is located just down the hall. Such a heavy burden of additional work will inevitably lead to anxiety, frustration, and burnout for both mentor and mentee.

It is paradoxical that mentoring, once urged by universities to help insure the quality of new teachers, has become a substitute for university education in a growing number of states.

THE NATIONAL COUNCIL FOR ACCREDITATION OF TEACHER EDUCATION (NCATE)

Four standards promulgated by the National Council for Accreditation of Teacher Education (2009) are as follows:

Standard 1: *Candidate Knowledge, Skills, and Professional Dispositions*
Candidates preparing to work in schools as teachers or other school professionals know and demonstrate the content knowledge, pedagogical content knowledge and skills, pedagogical and professional knowledge and skills, and professional dispositions necessary to help all students learn. Assessments indicate that candidates meet professional, state, and institutional standards . . .

Standard 3: *Field Experiences and Clinical Practice*
The unit and its school partners design, implement, and evaluate field experiences and clinical practice so that teacher candidates and other school professionals develop and demonstrate the knowledge, skills, and professional dispositions necessary to help all students learn.

Standard 4: *Diversity*
The unit designs, implements, and evaluates curriculum and provides experiences for candidates to acquire and demonstrate the knowledge, skills, and professional dispositions necessary to help all students learn. Assessments indicate that candidates can demonstrate and apply proficiencies related to diversity. Experiences provided for candidates include working with diverse populations, including higher education and P–12 school faculty, candidates, and students in P–12 schools.

Standard 5: *Faculty Qualifications, Performance, and Development*
Faculty are qualified and model best professional practices in scholarship, service, and teaching, including the assessment of their own effectiveness

as related to candidate performance. They also collaborate with colleagues in the disciplines and schools. The unit systematically evaluates faculty performance and facilitates professional development.

While these standards may seem logical and even obvious, emerging programs at many universities do not assess dispositions or skills, do not require field experiences or clinical practice, do not require monitoring diversity among their teachers or K–12 field experiences, and do not consider the qualifications of individuals who actually deliver the program. Increasingly, colleges of education are experimenting with ways to circumvent accreditation standards so that they can compete with cut-rate offerings aggressively marketed by corporations.

Thus, a university may seek NCATE-accreditation for its on-campus master's degree, but not for its online master's degree. In this way, universities are trying to survive by concurrently offering two separate and unequal programs: one that meets certain standards of quality, and a second that is profitable.

It would seem to be a matter of time until state departments of education, accrediting agencies, and university central administrators get uncomfortable with the realization that while accredited programs struggle to enroll a hundred students, unaccredited, online programs are enrolling thousands.

Does an institution or business that routinely produces the majority of its new teachers in unaccredited programs deserve to be accredited? NCATE still accredits by program, so an institution can be accredited in undergraduate math middle grades, but not in any other program. Although the university can proclaim "NCATE-accredited" on its website, its undergraduate math middle grades program may enroll 4 students, while its online, graduate certification program may enroll 1,004.

CONCLUSION

At the beginning of this chapter, I noted that the history of teacher-preparation programs has always vacillated between two philosophies:

1. Attracting academically accomplished individuals to the profession
2. Educating whoever wants to teach to become a teacher

Of course, these two philosophies are not mutually exclusive. It is possible to have both highly accomplished and well-educated teachers, and several colleges of education located in research universities currently enjoy this distinction. Unfortunately, while the quality of teachers graduating from such institutions is high, the number of teachers graduating from them is small, in fact a trickle, especially in comparison to the flood of teachers being produced in "Walmart-university" and quick-and-easy alternative environments.

High-quality teacher preparation is available now; the problem is that teacher certification has become market-driven, not quality-driven. As a result, many new teachers are not the best they can be. Instead, they are the products of a system that has made them the cheapest they can be.

Chapter Four

Teacher Certification around the World

The disintegration of teacher-certification programs in the United States holds an eerie similarity to the recent meltdown of American financial institutions. In 2000, Senator Phil Gramm helped pass the Commodity Futures Modernization Act, which allowed unregulated trading in financial instruments called derivatives. Recently, Gramm acknowledged that the advent of these new investment instruments created an environment "so opaque that nobody knew who was holding the bag" (Fox 2009).

Billionaire investment guru Warren Buffett (2002) has characterized derivatives as "financial weapons of mass destruction" and hypothesized that their proliferation will be responsible for the ruin of significant numbers of banks and financial firms over the next twenty years. Of course, no one purposefully set out to destroy America's financial infrastructure by promoting unfettered, unregulated trading in derivatives, but that is what has happened.

Similarly, the No Child Left Behind Act of 2001, whose purported purpose was to insure that all students get a highly qualified teacher (HQT), has had an unintentionally devastating effect on the quality of teacher preparation. No Child Left Behind defined an HQT as possessing three credentials:

- Bachelor's degree
- Certification to teach
- Proven knowledge of the subject taught

Few could argue against these well-intentioned requirements. However, the subsequent scramble to provide evidence for them has brought chaos and uncertainty to teacher preparation in the United States. Although the possession of a bachelor's degree is easy enough to verify, the issue of certification is more difficult. States under threat of financial reprisals by the federal government for not measuring up to its HQT statute have had to either promote higher enrollments in rigorous, university-based, NCATE-accredited programs or reconsider what was meant by *certification*.

Because state funding for higher education has been declining at the same time that enrollments have been climbing, most states have opted for the easier solution: redefining certification. Certification has come to mean the ability to pass a multiple-choice test—usually in the subject area. Across the United States, the two components—academic preparation and testing—have become separate entities.

There is a teacher-preparation program, and there is a test for certification. In most states, a student who fails in a teacher-preparation program, but passes the test, can still become a teacher. However, a student who passes a teacher-preparation program, but fails the test, cannot.

In most high-achieving countries, such as Singapore, Finland, Japan, and South Korea, testing and preparation are not separate but complementary components of the process of becoming a teacher. For example, a teacher in Singapore takes no test of legitimacy at the end of a program after he or she has already survived a rigorous admissions process, attended school for five years, and engaged in extensive practice teaching. Instead, the test in Singapore is at the front end of the admissions process, another data point for considering an applicant's potential as a teacher. All candidates take the same exam. In the United States, states use different tests and different cut-off scores, and the exam is given at the end of the program—not the beginning.

The differences in teacher preparation among countries are actually quite remarkable. Over the past decade in the United States, for example, teacher certification has become deregulated, privatized, and decentralized. During this same time period in the high-achieving countries of Singapore and Finland, teacher certification has become closely regulated, public, and centralized.

TEACHER PREPARATION IN SINGAPORE

Singapore is a large, diverse city-state of five million people located on the coast of China. Student scores from Singapore routinely are among the highest in international comparisons. Unlike the thousands of universities and businesses that certify teachers in the United States, only one entity in Singapore is permitted to prepare teachers: the National Institute for Education (NIE).

The NIE requires teacher candidates to be in the top third of their graduating class and to score well on a rigorous entrance-exam expressly designed for teachers. If candidates fulfill these two requirements, then they are interviewed to ascertain the extent to which their personal qualities are suited to the profession. If candidates make it through the admissions process (only one in five applicants is admitted), then they are allowed to take specialized courses in pedagogy and the content area, and to undertake a slate of increasingly more responsible field experiences. In the field experiences, candidates are assigned mentors from both the NIE and a school. When a student graduates from the NIE, they are allowed to competitively interview for teaching positions.

The first years are probationary for the newly hired Singapore teacher. The new teacher is assigned a reduced load and is guided by a small army of experienced personnel, including a "teacher buddy," a mentor, a subject-area specialist, a grade-level specialist, and a department chair. At any point during the probationary period, a teacher may be counseled out of the profession, especially if performance is subpar or improvement has been unsatisfactory.

Teachers are offered a straightforward career ladder in Singapore, and promotions are based in large part upon the performance of their students. Unlike the United States, though, Singapore's career ladder is dependent upon teacher performance, not years of service. Only a small percentage of Singapore teachers meet the qualifications to move up to the next higher level each year.

Singapore teachers are expected to attend at least one hundred hours of professional development per year, and the government contributes funds annually to help defray expenses. In contrast, many states in the United States have reduced or eliminated professional-development requirements. In fact, in Texas, Georgia, Florida, and other states, teachers receive little to no increments in pay for any kind of professional development, including advanced degrees. In these states, a PhD in physics is worth little more than a BS in physical education.

The trend in the United States is the development of policies to count related work—such as performing extra duties (supervising children during their lunch, for example) or updating curriculum—as professional development. Individual states' modest requirements for professional development have diminished over time. In most states today, the total requirement for professional development is the equivalent of six hours of college credit every five to ten years.

Singapore requires teachers to complete more than twice as many hours of professional development in a single year, but it also provides teachers with time, money, and freedom to select the professional-development opportunities of their choice.

More recently, emphasis in Singapore has been on educating the "whole child." A framework known as VSK (Values, Skills, and Knowledge) has put an emphasis on "future-oriented teachers who are adaptable and flexible to meet the uncertain demands of a changing environment. The VSK model emphasized inquiry, innovation, reflection, mutual respect, personal connections, collaboration and community" (United Nations Educational, Scientific and Cultural Organization 2007). In other words, the VSK framework acknowledges the importance of attitude and the development of character.

Perhaps the most intriguing aspect of the Singapore system is that the government pays the tuition and fees of prospective teachers. In fact, in addition to free tuition and fees, the government issues a generous monthly stipend. However, if a candidate fails to make it all the way through the program, or quits teaching before fulfilling the requisite amount of time (usually five to eight years), he or she must return all funds spent on his or her education.

Singapore also has a unique program to lure recently retired, former master teachers out of retirement to teach. In a recent year, the program brought back to the classroom almost 1,400 teachers (Shanmugaratnam 2006).

TEACHER CERTIFICATION IN FINLAND

As in Singapore, teacher preparation is highly regulated in Finland. Laws dictate specific rules as well as the general outline of programs to be offered through universities. For example, all elementary and secondary teachers in Finland are required to obtain a master's degree, which in most cases is attainable in five years.

Half of a student's teacher-preparation program is devoted to study of major and minor subject areas, 20 percent involves pedagogic studies, 25 percent consists of electives, and 5 percent involves linguistics and communications (Program for International Student Achievement 2009). Extensive field experiences with progressively more responsible teaching experiences are a hallmark of Finland's preparation system.

Finland also has polytechnic academies (offering the equivalent of a vocational education in the United States) for secondary students. Teacher preparation for polytechnic schools is also tightly managed, and like teachers in the academic schools, prospective teachers at a polytechnic academy must obtain a master's degree in the subject area to be qualified to teach.

Finland has teacher unions, tenure, merit pay, and a highly competitive admissions system for teachers. As in Singapore, all prospective teachers must post impressive grades on their academic work, demonstrate a proclivity for working with children, and score well on entrance exams even before applying for admission to teacher-preparation programs. Of the many that apply, only around 13 percent of applicants are accepted (Finland Ministry of Education 2009).

As in Singapore, teachers in Finland are offered abundant professional-development opportunities. Class size in Finland averages eighteen students, and classes at the secondary level are forty-five minutes long with fifteen minutes between periods—quite a contrast to the United States, where classes of thirty students rush to go to the bathroom and return in the allotted five-minute interval between classes.

Although Finland has a national curriculum, teachers have great latitude in choosing what to teach and how to teach. Incredibly, teachers are not evaluated by administrators, nor are schools ranked. In fact, student and school performance are not published for public consumption at all. Instead, the data is privately shared with individual students and schools to help them improve. Quite the radical innovation.

Another interesting fact about Finland is that its student scores on international tests were, at best, middling a few decades ago. To invigorate its K–12 schools, Finland embarked on major school reform, which included upgrading expectations for teachers. The country wrested control of teacher education from disparate providers and moved all teacher-preparation programs to universities, where they remain today.

TEACHER CERTIFICATION IN THE UNITED STATES

In contrast to Finland and Singapore, whose central agencies administer tight control over teacher preparation, more than 1,200 institutions prepare teachers in the United States. Add to this number the burgeoning industries in alternative certification represented by businesses, state agencies, and K–12 schools, and the number of places where a teacher might be prepared approaches 2,000. Requirements for admission, standards of achievement, and certification processes vary not only by state, but also by the certifying agency (university, business, school district, community college, or department of education).

Much like the complex derivatives of high finance, whose values are sometimes impossible to discern, teacher certification in the United States leaves us unsure who is preparing teachers, how well teachers are being prepared, or how many teachers are being prepared. Although the laws associated with Title II were supposed to insure reporting of such data, enforcement guidelines are weak or nonexistent. Thus, many state departments of education have no idea how many teachers are becoming alternatively certified and have no intention of trying to keep track of it.

Another area where the United States differs from the academically highest-scoring OECD (Organization for Economic Cooperation and Development) countries is with regard to professional development. In most high-scoring countries, professional development for teachers is a priority, and expectations are that a teacher will continually develop his or her intellect and teaching repertoire over the span of a career.

While the United States is rapidly decentralizing certification and allowing teacher preparation to become a profit-center for business, countries such as Singapore and Finland are tightening controls on teacher preparation and focusing upon unprofitable goals, such as the overall welfare of the child. In international tests, scores of students in the United States are consistently in the middle to bottom half while scores of students from Singapore and Finland are at the top.

SCHOOLS AS AGENTS OF SOCIAL CHANGE

It seems illogical that a strict regimen of standardized testing could be considered an antidote to the social problems of the poor and the disenfranchised, but the No Child Left Behind Act gained widespread, bipartisan political support through precisely this logic. School reform in the United States largely has been contained at the K–12 level and has focused upon the establishment of measurable outcomes: setting curricular standards, specifying student outcomes, integrating technology, and (if that were not enough already) certifying teachers willing to play by these rules.

In the meantime, other countries have taken a broader approach. While American schools spend billions on testing and more testing, other countries are earmarking funds for tax incentives to make staying at home with children more attractive for at least one parent and to create more child-friendly environments at schools.

There are many ways to respond to the evidence that some American teachers are burned out, struggling, and ineffective. However, to prescribe a remedy that makes admission into teacher preparation easy, preparation facile, and professional development superfluous seems absurd. In response to poor student performance and apathetic student attitudes, America has decided to improve performance by requiring every prospective teacher to take a multiple-choice exam in the content area?

POVERTY AND ACHIEVEMENT

Three dubious distinctions characterize America's poorest students: most hail from one- or no-parent households, they are the least healthy children in the country, and they score at the very bottom of achievement tests. The following table depicts the percentage of students in Finland, Australia, and the United States who scored at or below level 1 on the Program for International Student Assessment (PISA; 1 is the lowest possible score on PISA, and 6 is the highest).

Finland's children are difficult to find among the poorest-performing students on PISA's tests. Only 5 percent or so of Finnish students struggle at this lowest level of achievement. Compared to Finland's

Table 4.1.   Percentage of students performing at level 1 or lower on PISA (2006)

	Reading	*Mathematics*	*Science*
Finland	5	6	4
Australia	14	13	13
United States	Data removed	28	24

Source: Program for International Student Achievement 2007.

students, Australia's students are more abundant among the poorest performers, with 13–14 percent of its fifteen-year-olds performing at the lowest level.

While Australian achievement seems worrisome when matched against Finland's performance, Australia is doing quite well in comparison with America. In the United States, approximately one out of four students scores at the lowest-possible level (or below) in mathematics and science. Although scores on reading would reflect a similar pattern, data on reading among American students was recently removed from PISA.

Interestingly, the poverty rate in Finland is 5 percent, which is roughly equivalent to the percentage of students performing at the lowest levels. Similarly, the poverty rate in Australia is 13 percent, or roughly equivalent to the number of students performing at the lowest level. In the United States, the poverty rate is around 12 percent, but twice as many American students score at level 1 or lower on achievement tests.

From this data, one can infer that America is not only doing a poor job of educating students in poverty, it also is failing to educate significant numbers of the nonpoor. In recent decades, underachievement in America has been wholly perceived as a school problem, and solutions have focused solely on interactions with students during school hours.

The latest thinking in the United States is not toward more family-friendly policies or broader social initiatives or higher-quality teacher preparation, but toward more frequent testing for students and a loosening of certification requirements for teachers. To become a teacher in Singapore, Finland, Hong Kong, and other high-achieving countries, candidates are required to

• be among the top performers in their class and pass through a strict admissions regimen,

- complete five or more years of course work and field experiences,
- obtain a master's degree before starting as a full-time teacher, and
- continually pursue professional development.

To become a teacher in America, candidates are required to

- satisfy few, if any, admissions requirements,
- complete no courses or field experiences prior to full-time teaching,
- obtain a bachelor's degree in any field from any institution, and
- engage in no or minimal professional development.

Undeniably, the largest and fastest-growing teacher-preparation programs in the United States offer the totality of their preparation programs in five weeks or less. These programs are open to all individuals holding a bachelor's degree in almost any subject area. Once hired, these individuals are on their own, often without the support of seasoned teachers or administrative staff.

Little wonder that American students are not competing well with students from other countries.

CONCLUSION

High-achieving countries, such as Finland and Singapore, have centralized control over teacher preparation. Aspiring teachers in Finland and Singapore must be at the top of their class and must successfully complete programs of graduate study specially designed for teachers. In many ways, teacher-preparation programs in Finland and Singapore are similar to the better programs at research universities in the United States.

Professional development for teachers is well-supported, relevant, and continuous for teachers in Singapore and Finland, while in the United States, professional development for teachers is minimal or nonexistent. In the United States, in fact, some states do not recognize the attainment of graduate degrees. In some states, a teacher with a PhD in physics receives the same pay as a teacher with a BS in physical education.

Data from international tests indicates that high-achieving countries, such as Finland and Singapore, have perhaps 5 percent of their students scoring at the lowest levels. In the United States, 25 percent of students score at the lowest levels.

It is an absurd proposition that uneducated, inexperienced teachers will somehow help raise student achievement in the United States, yet teacher-preparation policy for the past few decades has followed precisely this logic.

Chapter Five

Ethics and the Lack of Ethics

As with standards for teacher certification, rules of conduct for teachers vary by state, or in some cases, by city or school. While the American Medical Association has developed a code of ethics for doctors, and the American Bar Association has developed standards of conduct for lawyers, no national teacher organization exists to promulgate a code of ethics for teachers.

The closest facsimile of a national code of ethics for teachers was developed in 1975 by the National Education Association (NEA). However, many teachers are not members of the NEA and the organization has little visibility in many areas of the country. Nevertheless, the NEA code of ethics still shows up in state documents and on department of education websites from time to time.

For example, in attempting to locate a contemporary code of ethics for California teachers, the only ethics to be found are the old 1975 NEA standards. New Mexico's code of ethics for teachers features many NEA standards verbatim, but it also includes modified NEA standards and rules unique to the state of New Mexico. Similarly, the NEA's standards show up in accreditation reports for colleges of education, and in codes of ethics for private, religious schools.

An Internet search on a particular sentence in the standards, such as "The educator therefore works to stimulate the spirit of inquiry, the acquisition of knowledge and understanding, and the thoughtful formulation of worthy goals," reveals thousands of documents using various parts of the standards, though they rarely attribute authorship to the NEA. The NEA standards are neither long nor complex. They consist of three parts:

a preamble, a section on commitment to students, and a section on professionalism.

Preamble

The educator, believing in the worth and dignity of each human being, recognizes the supreme importance of the pursuit of truth, devotion to excellence, and the nurture of the democratic principles. Essential to these goals is the protection of freedom to learn and to teach and the guarantee of equal educational opportunity for all. The educator accepts the responsibility to adhere to the highest ethical standards.

The educator recognizes the magnitude of the responsibility inherent in the teaching process. The desire for the respect and confidence of one's colleagues, of students, of parents, and of the members of the community provides the incentive to attain and maintain the highest possible degree of ethical conduct. The Code of Ethics of the Education Profession indicates the aspiration of all educators and provides standards by which to judge conduct.

The remedies specified by the NEA and/or its affiliates for the violation of any provision of this Code shall be exclusive and no such provision shall be enforceable in any form other than the one specifically designated by the NEA or its affiliates.

Principle I
Commitment to the Student

The educator strives to help each student realize his or her potential as a worthy and effective member of society. The educator therefore works to stimulate the spirit of inquiry, the acquisition of knowledge and understanding, and the thoughtful formulation of worthy goals.

In fulfillment of the obligation to the student, the educator—

1. Shall not unreasonably restrain the student from independent action in the pursuit of learning.
2. Shall not unreasonably deny the student's access to varying points of view.
3. Shall not deliberately suppress or distort subject matter relevant to the student's progress.
4. Shall make reasonable effort to protect the student from conditions harmful to learning or to health and safety.

5. Shall not intentionally expose the student to embarrassment or disparagement.
6. Shall not on the basis of race, color, creed, sex, national origin, marital status, political or religious beliefs, family, social, or cultural background, or sexual orientation, unfairly—
   a. Exclude any student from participation in any program
   b. Deny benefits to any student
   c. Grant any advantage to any student
7. Shall not use professional relationships with students for private advantage.
8. Shall not disclose information about students obtained in the course of professional service unless disclosure serves a compelling professional purpose or is required by law.

Principle II
Commitment to the Profession

The education profession is vested by the public with a trust and responsibility requiring the highest ideals of professional service.

In the belief that the quality of the services of the education profession directly influences the nation and its citizens, the educator shall exert every effort to raise professional standards, to promote a climate that encourages the exercise of professional judgment, to achieve conditions that attract persons worthy of the trust to careers in education, and to assist in preventing the practice of the profession by unqualified persons.

In fulfillment of the obligation to the profession, the educator—

1. Shall not in an application for a professional position deliberately make a false statement or fail to disclose a material fact related to competency and qualifications.
2. Shall not misrepresent his/her professional qualifications.
3. Shall not assist any entry into the profession of a person known to be unqualified in respect to character, education, or other relevant attribute.
4. Shall not knowingly make a false statement concerning the qualifications of a candidate for a professional position.
5. Shall not assist a noneducator in the unauthorized practice of teaching.
6. Shall not disclose information about colleagues obtained in the course of professional service unless disclosure serves a compelling professional purpose or is required by law.
7. Shall not knowingly make false or malicious statements about a colleague.

8. Shall not accept any gratuity, gift, or favor that might impair or appear to influence professional decisions or action (National Education Association 2009a).

If the NEA standards were strictly adhered to by states today, five-week alternative certification programs would not exist, nor would quick-and-easy preparation programs at universities. After all, the purpose of those kinds of programs is to put a warm body in the classroom immediately with as little course work and as little field work as possible.

The NEA code of ethics specifically states that part of the job of a teacher is to "assist in preventing the practice of the profession by unqualified persons." Due to recently passed legislation in several states, however, a teacher is compelled to serve as mentor to "unqualified persons" at the administrator's request.

Although there is much to recommend the NEA's standards with regard to maintaining teacher quality, they have remained untouched and relatively out of sight for more than thirty years. In contrast to the dormancy of discussion about a national code of ethics for teachers, medicine and law have recently spent significant money, time, and energy on updating national guidelines for ethics in the twenty-first century.

The American Bar Association's *Annotated Model Rules of Professional Conduct*, updated in 2007, runs 710 pages while the American Medical Association's *Code of Medical Ethics: Current Opinions with Annotations, 2008–2009*, updated in 2008, runs 504 pages (American Bar Association 2007; American Medical Association 2008). Both books contain detailed rules and examples of conduct that would constitute violation of the rules. Indeed, any doctor or lawyer who breaks these established rules of conduct may face repercussions, such as loss of license or criminal prosecution.

Because no uniform, national code of ethics exists for American teachers, what might be considered unethical in one setting might be considered inconsequential someplace else. For example, Alabama's code of ethics states that it is unethical for a teacher at a school event to be "under the influence of, possessing, or consuming alcoholic beverages or using tobacco" (Alabama Department of Education 2009a).

Like Alabama, Georgia explicitly restricts the consumption of alcohol by teachers at school events, but Georgia offers no restrictions on smoking. So it would be unethical for a teacher to smoke a cigarette at a high-school prom in Alabama, but smoking would be acceptable at a prom in Georgia.

In perusing state codes of ethics, we find that the terms *truth*, *values*, *democracy*, *citizenship*, and *excellence* are used repeatedly, though these words can be difficult to define, let alone monitor.

States fall into one of four categories regarding codes of ethics:

1. They have officially or unofficially adopted the NEA's 1975 code of ethics.
2. They recognize no code of ethics for teachers.
3. They have purposefully not developed a code of ethics for teachers because they want school districts or communities to develop their own, local codes of ethics.
4. They have developed and ratified a state-centric code of ethics.

Like California, the states of Kansas, Wyoming, and Tennessee use the NEA's 1975 formulation as their code of ethics, at least unofficially. Arizona has adopted no code of ethics for teachers, though its state legislature recently considered a bill that would have made the expression of political or religious beliefs by a teacher during class hours a violation of state law. The bill would have made it justifiable for principals to fire a teacher who might respond to the question "Who did you vote for?" while at school.

Like Arizona, Virginia has no code of ethics for teachers. Maryland, Nevada, South Carolina, and New Hampshire have no code of ethics either, but the states claim that the oversight is purposeful. They contend that the power to set standards of ethical behavior should belong to schools and communities and not the state.

Among the states that have ratified a code of ethics for teachers, Vermont and New York have formulated commendable documents. The Vermont code is a brief but eloquent statement of beliefs that includes the altruistic sentiment that teachers should be "dedicated to compassionate service on behalf of our students and their families." While compassion is rarely acknowledged in standards or rules of conduct, it is what drives many teachers to remain in the profession.

The essential qualities of the competent and caring educator include moral integrity, humane attitudes, reflective practice, and a sound understanding of academic content and pedagogy. The public vests educators with trust and responsibility for educating the children of Vermont. We believe that fulfilling this charge requires educators to demonstrate the highest standards of ethical conduct.

We, as professional educators, respect the dignity and individuality of every human being. We are committed to, and model for our students, the lifelong pursuit of learning and academic excellence. We are dedicated to effective scholarly practice, further enhanced by collaboration with colleagues and those in the greater educational community. Furthermore, we are dedicated to compassionate service on behalf of our students and their families and advocate for them in the school and community settings.

We recognize and accept both the public trust and the magnitude of responsibility inherent in our profession. To this end, we put forth this statement of beliefs as the foundation for ethical practice for all Vermont educators to honor and follow (Vermont Department of Education 2009a).

Like Vermont, New York has developed a state-centric, distinctive set of standards of conduct for teachers. New York's code is remarkable in that it manages to convey the diverse constituencies with which a teacher routinely works (students, parents, colleagues, administrators, community members, professionals with similar curricular interests) while making clear that the focus for a professional should be on the development of the whole child. In its emphasis on the whole child, New York's code is similar to Singapore's recent efforts to reemphasize the importance of dispositions through a new curriculum called VSK (Values, Skills, and Knowledge; see chapter 4).

The *New York State Code of Ethics for Educators* has elaborations, but the basic six principles are as follows:

- Principle 1: Educators nurture the intellectual, physical, emotional, social, and civic potential of each student.
- Principle 2: Educators create, support, and maintain challenging learning environments for all.
- Principle 3: Educators commit to their own learning in order to develop their practice.

- Principle 4: Educators collaborate with colleagues and other professionals in the interest of student learning.
- Principle 5: Educators collaborate with parents and community, building trust and respecting confidentiality.
- Principle 6: Educators advance the intellectual and ethical foundation of the learning community (New York State Education Department 2009a).

To show the great variability in standards governing teacher ethics in the United States, excerpts from codes of ethics of selected states are featured below. The first date in parenthesis indicates when the code was ratified or last updated.

In Arkansas, unethical conduct includes "unreasonably denying students access to varying points of view." Ethical conduct includes "modeling for students and colleagues the responsible use of public property" (2008; Arkansas Department of Education 2007).

Connecticut teachers are expected to "guide students to acquire the requisite skills and understanding for participatory citizenship and to realize their obligation to be worthy and contributing members of society" (2003; Connecticut State Department of Education 2007).

Delaware's *Professional Standards Board's Ethical Guideline for Delaware Educators* is unique for its acknowledgement of the roles of family and community: "The educator shall communicate appropriate information with parents and endeavor to understand their community's cultures and diverse home environments" (2009; Professional Standards Board 2009).

Similarly, Kentucky acknowledges that a teacher should "endeavor to understand community cultures and diverse home environments of students" (2009; Kentucky Education Professional Standards Board 2006).

Although it might be difficult for a teacher to know ahead of time what conditions might be detrimental to a student's mental health, Florida's code requires that the teacher have the prescience to "make reasonable effort to protect the student from conditions harmful . . . to the student's mental and/or physical health and/or safety" (1998; Florida Department of Education

2009a). Although most teachers are experts in recognizing and nullifying threats, being able to protect students from conditions that might lead to impairment of mental health is a bit more challenging. For example, the teaching of evolution might be considered harmful to a child whose parents believe in creationism.

The Hawaii Teacher Standards Board (2009a) code of ethics advocates that teachers be honest with "students, parents, colleagues, and the public." Does this mean replacing euphemistic phrases commonly used with parents such as "Your son is very social" with "Your son has talked nonstop since the first day of class"?

Idaho's code of ethics explicitly forbids a teacher from "taking inappropriate pictures (digital, photographic or video) of students" and from "taking inappropriate pictures (digital, photographic or video) of colleagues" (2009; Idaho Department of Education 2009a).

Iowa's lengthy code of ethics notes that a teacher's license will be revoked if the teacher is found guilty of detaining a child in a brothel (2003; Iowa Board of Educational Examiners 2003).

Louisiana has a code of standards for educational leaders that includes the requirement of developing a mission statement. However, no code has been approved for teachers.

Perhaps because of the rural nature of the state, the *Maine Educators' Code of Ethics* suggests that teachers "should take an interest in undertakings that make for community betterment and, as far as practicable without interference with his professional duties, he should avail himself of opportunities to participate actively in the social and religious life of the community" (1994). Maine's code of ethics also addresses teacher pay, hiring practices, and student-teacher supervision.

Massachusetts's *Regulations for Educator Licensure and Preparation Program Approval* contains several ethics clauses, including rules that allow districts to dismiss a teacher for not teaching to the sanctioned "content standards of the relevant curriculum frameworks" (2007; Massachusetts Department of Elementary and Secondary Education 2009a).

The writers of the Minnesota code of ethics seemed to have one eye toward weak, alternative certification programs when they wrote that "a teacher shall accept a contract for a teaching position that requires licensing only if properly or provisionally licensed for that position" (2003; Minnesota Board of Teaching 2003).

Mississippi, the state with thousands of teachers emanating from some of the weakest alternative certification programs in the world, paradoxically, has a strict, lengthy, sophisticated code of ethics—but only for administrators. There is no code of ethics for teachers.

Missouri's code of ethics includes explicit language promoting the independence and decision-making powers of teachers, such as:

- We believe academic freedom is inherent in, and essential to, the teaching profession.
- We believe that for students to learn, teachers must be free to teach.
- We believe every educator should have a broad general education, a depth of preparation in special areas and a mastery of knowledge and skills.
- We believe the purpose of education is to develop each individual for his or her fullest participation in the American democratic society, to pursue truth and to seek excellence. We will accept the responsibility of taking the initiative to eliminate all barriers that prevent full access to this unique education for all (Missouri State Teachers Association 2009).

Despite such glowing language, the Missouri legislature recently approved an alternative certification program (the American Board for Certification of Teacher Excellence [ABCTE]) that requires no course work, no field hours, and no major in education for new teachers.

Montana's code of ethics for teachers is interesting because, unlike most states' codes of ethics, it has no provisions that address the need to acknowledge and respect different cultures and various points of view (Certification Standards and Practices Advisory Council 1997).

Nebraska's code of ethics for teachers explicitly forbids a teacher from using corporal punishment (1967; Nebraska Professional Practices Commission 1967).

New Jersey's code of ethics includes provisions to boost a teacher's ego: "Each staff member shall be expected to perform his assigned duties with the highest regard for the ethical and moral standards of his profession, craft, or trade, in a manner that shall enhance the image and stature of himself" (1988; Center for the Study of Ethics in the Professions 2009).

Pennsylvania has a nicely worded statement on how diversity might influence instructional strategies: "Professional educators shall accept the value of diversity in educational practice. Diversity requires educators to have a range of methodologies and to request the necessary tools for effective teaching and learning" (2008; Professional Standards and Practices Commission 1992).

The *Rhode Island Educator Code of Professional Responsibility* is a simple declaration of five principles that couches ethics in terms of responsibilities to students, self, colleagues, parents and community, and (surprise!) the Rhode Island Board of Regents (Rhode Island Department of Elementary and Secondary Education 2009).

South Dakota's code of ethics contains some interesting provisions related to relationships with colleagues. A teacher should "not interfere with a colleague's exercise of political and citizenship rights and responsibilities" nor should a teacher "interfere with the free participation of colleagues in the affairs of their associations" (2001; South Dakota Department of Education 2008).

Texas, home to an explosion of alternatively certified teachers, many of whom are licensed through corporate-run Internet programs, has few references to the development of the intellect in its code of ethics. Texas's code includes such statements as "The Texas educator, in maintaining the dignity of the profession, shall respect and obey the law, demonstrate personal integrity, and exemplify honesty" (2002; State Board for Educator Certification 2002). Of course honesty is essential, but shouldn't a teacher help a student develop his or her intellect?

In Utah, the code of ethics gives school districts wide latitude to dismiss teachers. Offenses that could lead to firing include the commission of a misdemeanor, acts of emotional abuse, stalking, "exceeding the prescribed dosages of prescription medications while at school," and promoting "athletic camps, summer leagues, travel opportunities, or other outside instructional opportunities from which the educator receives personal remuneration" (2009; Utah State Board of Education 2009).

Washington's *Standard V* includes several statements on monitoring the extent to which a teacher's instruction aligns with state standards. For example, one rule requires teachers to "positively impact student learning that is aligned with curriculum standards and outcomes," and another requires that a teacher's instruction be "informed by standards-based assessment" (2007; Professional Educator Standards Board 2009). Such requirements would seem more at home in a curriculum guide than a code of ethics.

West Virginia's *Employee Code of Conduct* covers the rules for educators in the state and includes attention to appearance and reliability. Teachers in West Virginia should "exhibit professional behavior by showing positive examples of preparedness, communication, fairness, punctuality, attendance, language, and appearance" (2002; West Virginia Department of Education 2009b).

Wisconsin's code of teacher ethics includes strong language relative to a teacher's political beliefs, such as "The teacher should exercise his/her full rights as a citizen but he/she should avoid controversies which may tend to decrease his/her value as a teacher" (1991). The assurance that a teacher deserves the same rights as any citizen is a concept that lawmakers in Arizona might consider.

Most professions have codes of ethics by which all of their members must abide. However, as with alternative certification programs, there seems to be little consistency among codes of ethics across states. But are ethics for teachers really so malleable? Is there a community in the United States where public drunkenness, sex with a minor, and bribery would be considered ethical behavior for a teacher? Is there a state where compassion, intelligence, and diligence would be considered unethical behavior for a teacher?

While medicine and law have extensive codes of ethics, their professional organizations rarely charge members of their profession with unethical behavior. For example, a doctor routinely pays heavy insurance fees, and indeed, when a malpractice suit is filed, whether it is legitimate or not, the insurance company takes care of it.

The doctor continues practicing until the insurance company loses a series of malpractice suits and a pattern of incompetence or irresponsibility is revealed. Then someone must decide to expend the time and energy to see that the case goes to the American Medical Association (AMA), which will render a decision. Even if a case goes all the way to the AMA, there is a good chance that the doctor will continue practicing.

Similarly, in order for a lawyer to get disbarred by the American Bar Association (ABA), the misbehavior must be flagrant and habitual. Lawyers are rarely disbarred by the ABA.

The paradoxical nature of professional organizations is that they are supposed to serve their constituents while they simultaneously police them. Members pay dues to belong to the organization, and in return, the organization promises fealty and aid in times of trouble.

So it is understandable that these organizations are reticent to seek out misbehaving members. An individual joins a professional organization expecting support—not prosecution.

One of the consistent criticisms of the National Education Association (NEA) is that it does nothing to help identify weak teachers and to get them out of the classroom. In this regard, the NEA is no different from the AMA or the ABA. The first obligation of professional organizations is to protect their members.

In examining the myriad codes of ethics or absence of codes of ethics as the case may be, there appears to be no correlation between the length of a code and its clarity or power. In fact, some of the most powerful codes of ethics—from Vermont and New York—are also the shortest.

In 2001, the AMA adopted a *Declaration of Professional Responsibility: Medicine's Social Contract with Humanity* (American Medical Association 2009a). The declaration is eloquent, lucid, and unabashedly humanistic—three traits that are oddly missing in the codes of ethics for teachers in many states. I will close this chapter by citing adaptations of the nine principles of the declaration. Five of the principles are directly relevant to teaching and presented verbatim; four principles have been reworded from the original text to better fit the profession of teaching.

DECLARATION

We, the members of the world community of educators [original text: *physicians*], solemnly commit ourselves to:

1. Respect human life and the dignity of every individual. [No adaptation needed]

2. Refrain from supporting or committing crimes against humanity and condemn all such acts. [No adaptation needed]
3. Treat all students with competence and compassion and without prejudice. [Original text: *Treat the sick and injured with competence and compassion and without prejudice.*]
4. Apply our knowledge and skills when needed, though doing so may put us at risk. [No adaptation needed]
5. Protect the privacy and confidentiality of those for whom we care and breach that confidence only when keeping it would seriously threaten their health and safety or that of others. [No adaptation needed]
6. Work freely with colleagues to discover, develop, and promote advances in teaching that develop the intellect, promote cooperation, ameliorate suffering, and contribute to human well-being. [Original text: *Work freely with colleagues to discover, develop, and promote advances in medicine and public health that ameliorate suffering and contribute to human well-being.*]
7. Educate the public and polity about present and future threats to rational thought, tolerance, and the collective good. [Original text: *Educate the public and polity about present and future threats to the health of humanity.*]
8. Advocate for social, economic, educational, and political changes that promote the development of the intellect, promote cooperation, ameliorate suffering, and contribute to human well-being. [Original text: *Advocate for social, economic, educational, and political changes that ameliorate suffering and contribute to human well-being.*]
9. Teach and mentor those who follow us for they are the future of our caring profession. [No adaptation needed]

A comparable code of ethics would seem essential for the teaching profession to progress into the twenty-first century and beyond.

CONCLUSION

As with minimum scores on competency tests and the quality of teacher-preparation programs, no national standard for ethics exists for teachers.

Codes of ethics in states may be categorized in one of four ways, as follows:

1. They have officially or unofficially adopted the NEA's 1975 code of ethics.
2. They recognize no code of ethics for teachers.
3. They have purposefully not developed a code of ethics for teachers because they want school districts or communities to develop their own local codes of ethics.
4. They have developed and ratified a state-centric code of ethics.

As a result, what may be construed as unethical in one state may well be considered ethical in another. In states that allow communities to decide upon their own codes of conduct, what constitutes moral behavior may differ from school to school.

Unlike education, the professions of medicine and law have formulated detailed, exhaustive, national codes of ethics. However, while codes of conduct in medicine and law have high visibility within their professions, there is little visibility of ethics for teachers until an obvious breach occurs, such as a teacher physically abusing a student.

One of the paradoxes of professional organizations is that they are expected to simultaneously protect and police their membership. While law and medicine have impressive codes of ethics, their professional organizations by their nature are reluctant to prosecute dues-paying members.

The NEA has a much larger membership than either the ABA or the AMA, but the organization's track record of support for high-quality teacher-preparation programs has been dismal. High-quality teacher preparation is currently a low priority at the NEA.

Chapter Six

Doctor, Lawyer, Plumber, Undertaker, Teacher

Recently when I went to the doctor for my annual check-up, I spent over an hour in the reception area of the office, waiting amidst a throng of coughing and sneezing patients and a pile of outdated magazines. Eventually a nurse walked in and announced my name. I followed her down a long hallway to a small room where I waited another ten minutes.

The nurse returned, checked my blood pressure, asked me to step on a scale to get my weight, made a note of my height, and asked me several questions about my health. She left after a few minutes and reassured me that the doctor would eventually drop by. I waited another twenty minutes.

Finally the doctor knocked on the door and entered. The doctor appeared to be a fastidiously attired, slightly frazzled man in his fifties. He spoke to me gruffly and perfunctorily for about two minutes. Then he left the room.

I got dressed, walked down the hall, and gave the cashier my medical identification card. I wrote a check for the $25 co-pay for my five minutes with the nurse and two minutes with the doctor. Later I discovered that the total cost of my visit was $320, or $160 per minute with the doctor. At that rate, my doctor was grossing around $9,600 per hour, which would mean that he earned more money before lunch than an average teacher would earn in an entire year.

Contrast the routine of the doctor in this real-life scenario with that of a typical teacher. While the doctor works individually with patients and arranges to see them on his schedule, the teacher works with multitudes of children on a preset, inflexible schedule, usually seven hours per day, five days per week.

The doctor's time is considered precious, and he or she is well paid for it; the teacher's time is considered expendable, and he or she receives a modest paycheck. It is not uncommon for a teacher to be asked to do additional tasks: lunch-hour supervision, hall monitoring, bus duty, detention-hall monitoring, coaching sports teams, sponsoring extracurricular activities. A doctor is rarely asked to take on additional tasks, such as those of a cashier or receptionist.

The doctor's opinions are assumed to be expert, and his or her knowledge highly specialized; the teacher's opinions are often questioned, and his or her expertise is often undermined by administrative action or legislative decree. How did these professions develop into what they have become today? Why do governments consistently set guidelines for teachers, but rarely dare to offer advice for how a doctor should practice?

It is instructive to note that, in eighteenth-century England, doctors existed on the fringe of respectability, and strived for legitimacy by selling their services to the wealthy. In the nineteenth century in the United States, the status of the medical profession was poor and the pay was low. At that time, anyone could become a doctor. Medical schools were abundant and they offered "easy terms and quick degrees" (Starr 1982, 63).

Today in the Soviet Union, a doctor and a teacher make comparable salaries. Doctors in Mexico, Poland, Hungary, Portugal, Greece, and Finland have incomes comparable with other professions, and make a fraction of the salaries of doctors in the United States. The elevation of careers in medicine in the United States over the past hundred years has been due, in part, to two related phenomena:

1. The rise of a strong, national organization for doctors, the American Medical Association
2. The belief that a doctor possesses specialized expertise that is beyond the knowledge base of most patients

These two phenomena—national organization and specialized expertise—will be discussed as they pertain to teaching.

NATIONAL ORGANIZATION

In terms of income, stature, and power, doctors in America rank at the top of the professions. The transformation of medicine from low status to high status in America has been due in no small part to the formation and continuing presence of the American Medical Association (AMA). Not only does the AMA actively monitor the supply and demand of doctors, it polices the training of doctors to insure that standards and quality remain high.

When new legislation is introduced at the local, state, or federal level that might involve doctors, the AMA is there to weigh in on the proceedings. Over the past fifty years or so, few policies that might impugn the sovereignty of doctors have made it past the initial committee level. The AMA shows little tolerance for external market forces, price controls, generic drug plans, or any legislation that would restrict the independence and inviolability of a doctor's power.

Perhaps surprisingly, only about 150,000 of America's 900,000 physicians belong to the AMA today. Other doctors belong to the National Physician's Association (NPA), specialized organizations, or no organization at all. Despite representing only a minority of doctors, however, the AMA continues to influence legislation and governmental oversight of medicine. In 2008, the AMA spent over twenty million dollars in lobbying efforts at the federal level (Ricciardelli 2009).

In contrast, the national organization for teachers, the National Education Association (NEA), asserts that its membership is approximately three million, or most of the teachers in the country, and twenty times the membership of the AMA. While the NEA participates in some lobbying efforts, it is less diligent about policing the preparation of teachers and insuring that quality remains high in the profession.

Indeed, the NEA's website displays a list of what it considers major pressing issues—the No Child Left Behind Act, professional pay, education funding, minority community outreach, dropout prevention, and achievement gaps—but there is nothing about teacher preparation anywhere (National Education Association 2009b). To locate any information about the NEA's stand on teacher preparation, one must diligently search the inside pages of the website. It turns out that teacher preparation is found under the subheading of Teacher Quality, and located alongside topics such as charter schools, college affordability, early childhood education, the American Recovery and Reinvestment Act, educator tax-relief, English language learners, the E-Rate Program, health-care reform, higher education, the Individuals with Disabilities Education Act/special education, pension protection, privatization, reading, rural schools, school safety, social-security offsets (GPO/WEP), union rights, and vouchers.

Some critics contend that the NEA has been slow to criticize quick-and-easy alternative certification programs because it is too busy trying to recruit all new hires as members.

While the AMA has repeatedly influenced legislative decisions on Medicaid, Medicare, franchised emergency clinics, and relationships with drug companies, the NEA has been relatively ineffective in influencing legislation. The list of initiatives that the NEA has lobbied against—merit pay, school vouchers, the simplistic accountability practices of the No Child Left Behind Act, the continuing disempowerment of teachers—are the very traits that have become the most prominent features of the teaching profession in the twenty-first century.

EXPERTISE

One of the weaknesses of teaching as a profession is that many Americans do not perceive that teachers possess any sort of specialized expertise. Indeed, parents are more likely to interact with teachers in disputations over grades than to congratulate them on the brilliance of their lessons. The recent emphasis by the federal government on scientifically based research, particularly with regard to the teaching of reading, would seem to be a step in the direction of trying to formalize the knowledge base of teaching.

Like patients displaying symptoms of a disease, students who are poor readers may demonstrate specific kinds of behavior that can be diagnosed. With adequate training in identifying problems, a teacher might be able to prescribe methods and materials that have proven to be successful in similar cases.

For example, if a poor reader squints when reading, there might be a standard protocol established whereby a teacher administers a vision test, checks the student's ability to distinguish spatial objects, and assesses the student's short-term memory. Over time, a teacher would gain familiarity with specific symptoms and would have some knowledge about the effectiveness of various interventions.

There is much that is attractive about the proposition of developing methodologies that have withstood the gauntlet of scientific experimentation. In fact, the proliferation of reading specialists or literacy coaches within schools is predicated upon this kind of model.

However, the use of science in teaching is fundamentally different than the use of science in medicine. While a doctor might base his diagnosis upon data gleaned from biological and chemical assessments, such as a blood test, a teacher must skate upon the surface by reading facial expressions, ascertaining emotions from actions, and making split-second decisions based upon incomplete information.

While the doctor is detached from the environment of his patients, the teacher is enmeshed in the environment of those he or she serves every day, sometimes all day, five days per week. Perhaps this is why scientifically based instruction may appear to be more of an ideal than a practicality for most teachers.

Rarely does a teacher have the luxury of certainties — no blood-pressure reading, no white blood cell count, no PSA (prostate-specific antigen) reading, no mammogram result. While a doctor might reflect on a patient's symptoms and possible treatments once all data has been gathered, a teacher must act immediately in real time, guided by experience and instinct.

The only data at a teacher's disposal are raw test scores, which may or may not serve as a genuine indication of student ability. While the variables in a standardized test score are manifold, there are relatively few ways to dispute a blood test. An individual's blood test will likely not fluctuate due to changes in motivation, environment, or the amount of time spent preparing for the test.

A teacher's knowledge base is constructed through study, observation, experience, and endless trial and error. Many research studies have found that one of the strongest variables related to student success is a teacher's years of experience (Allen 2003; Darling-Hammond et al. 2005; Murnane and Phillips 1981; Rivkin, Huanushek, and Kain 2005).

Rightly so. It takes years to understand what an adolescent really means when he or she says, "It wasn't so bad." Also, a teacher must be malleable enough to alter instructional strategies for different student populations. What appeals to a gifted and talented, advanced-placement class may not necessarily appeal to a class of remedial readers. What appeals to students in a rural school in Montana may not appeal to students in a charter school in downtown New Orleans.

So by its nature, a teacher's expertise is localized, age- and subject-specific, and is revealed most vividly in moments of spontaneity or high anxiety. For example, while an experienced teacher can detect a threat in a seemingly innocuous, random comment from one student to another, a neophyte teacher may not recognize a threat exists until a fight between the students actually erupts into violent fisticuffs.

The kind of expertise possessed by the best teachers is difficult to transfer into measurable criteria. Charting how well a student scores on exams over the course of a year is certainly one possible way of assessing a teacher's effectiveness. However, it may not be the most telling measure.

Another measure of a teacher's expertise might be the student's attitude toward the subject matter at the end of the term. After all, a student born today may live for one hundred years or more, and the time spent studying a particular subject area in school is usually fifty minutes per day. A teacher who can instill love of a particular subject matter may induce in students an incentive that could endure for the rest of their lives.

One of the problems with accountability systems for teachers is that success is narrowly defined. Basically, a teacher's value is based upon measurable gains in student achievement scores over the school year. However, achievement tests rarely measure a student's affability or drive, eloquence, poise and presence, ability to research and create, or disposition to write and think.

Thus, a teacher's expertise may not be readily apparent, even if student test scores are tracked from student to teacher in every classroom in the country.

Another problem with measuring a teacher's expertise is that it is often not technical or abstruse. For example, most nonteachers can easily grasp the nuances of the aforementioned example of the experienced teacher breaking up a fight before it happens. However, such is not the case when a doctor begins to explain the rudiments of cancer, a malignant neoplasm that may metastasize through the lymph or blood, and the genetics of cancer pathogenesis. Just to understand what cancer is may require some translation.

Thus when a doctor speaks, the listener understands that the doctor possesses knowledge that is both technical and exotic; when a teacher speaks, the listener encounters vocabulary and explanations that are neither technical nor exotic. A doctor's opinion conveys a certain authority and therefore demands respect, while a teacher's opinion, especially a new teacher's opinion, may convey little authority. Respect for a new teacher, in particular, is negotiable.

PREPARATION FOR TEACHING AS COMPARED TO PREPARATION FOR OTHER PROFESSIONS

There is no alternative certification program for individuals who want to become doctors, just as there is no alternative certification program for individuals who wish to become lawyers, plumbers, or funeral directors. These professions require academic preparation, practical experience, mentoring, and time spent as a beginner in the field before full-fledged status is given. The table below indicates the preparation necessary to attain membership in these professions.

To obtain a license in medicine, an individual must successfully complete eight years of schooling, pass the United States Medical Licensing Exam and possibly additional exams in the specialty area, then complete a three-to-eight-year residency. Becoming a lawyer involves seven years of schooling, a passing score on the bar exam, and extensive, hands-on experience as a clerk, researcher, and junior member of a law firm or governmental agency.

Only with years of service can a lawyer expect to move up the career ladder. To become a funeral director, an individual must complete a bachelor's degree, successfully complete a year or two of study in mortuary science, achieve a passing score on the National Board Exam, and fulfill a one- or two-year internship under the guidance of an expert.

Although plumbing is considered a trade, guidelines dictate that an individual must spend five to six years of full-time work under the supervision of an expert to attain the status of master plumber. In addition, the master plumber must pass two exams and satisfactorily complete specialized training.

The requirements for becoming a teacher in America through a university-based program at a research university, such as the University of Oklahoma, are less than required of doctors or lawyers, but comparable with requirements for funeral directors or master plumbers.

While doctors and lawyers require both more schooling and longer internships, funeral directors require about the same amount of schooling and

Table 6.1. Comparison of Preparation Required in Medicine, Law, Mortuary Science, Plumbing, and Teaching

Profession	Academic Preparation	Grade Point Average	Field Experience	Apprenticeship	Exam
Medicine (general practitioner)	8 years (4 years of college plus 4 years of medical school)	Usually a minimum of a 3.5 grade point average to get into medical school	Frequent labs and visits to hospitals during medical school	3–8 year internship (residency)	United States Medical Licensing Exam in three parts (during second and fourth years of medical school, and first year of residency)
Law	7 years (4 years of college plus 3 years of law school)	Grade point requirements vary by institution, but are a criteria for admission.	Extensive internships with law firms and governmental agencies	Varies by state; most lawyers begin in junior positions and work toward becoming partner (though most do not make partner)	LSAT for admission to law school; state bar exam to practice as a lawyer
Mortuary Science (funeral director; Ohio)	Bachelor's degree plus 1–2 years of courses in mortuary science	No statewide minimum grade point average	Integrated into specialized training	1–2 year internship after completion of graduate degree	National Board Exam

Plumbing	For a journeyman plumber, 32 hours in backflow-prevention device testing and 4 years experience as an apprentice	No minimum grade point average; courses are Pass/Fail.	Integrated into training with a master plumber	Journeyman: completion of 7,500 hours of training under direction of a licensed master plumber; master plumber: serve as journeyman for 2 years, and complete 3,700 hours of training under a master plumber	Written exam for journeyman plumber; written exam for master plumber
Teaching (traditional route; University of Oklahoma)	Bachelor's degree plus 1 to 2 semesters of graduate work focusing on education	3.0 overall grade point average for admission	Four field experiences	Semester-long student teaching	Oklahoma General Education Test (OGET), Oklahoma Professional Teaching Examination (OPTE), Oklahoma Subject Area Tests (OSAT)
Teaching (alternative route; Teach For America)	Bachelor's degree	No minimum grade point average	None	None	Varies by state

internship hours. Plumbing requires less formal-education, but it mandates a significant interval for the progression to full membership as master plumber: five to six years.

From table 6.1, one can clearly ascertain that the expectations for teachers seeking certification through alternative programs, such as Teach For America, are less than the expectations for doctors, lawyers, funeral directors, or plumbers. Plumbers must pass two exams, must spend time studying specialized material (such as backflow prevention), and must spend five to six years learning at the elbow of an expert before becoming full-fledged members of the trade.

Like plumbers, teachers seeking alternative certification may take two exams. But that is where the similarity ends. While plumbers spend five to six years studying plumbing at the elbow of an expert, Teach For America students, for example, spend five weeks participating in a "cram session" during the summer when there are few children around to teach. After five weeks, Teach For America students begin their jobs, with pay and status equal to "master teachers," who may have been teaching for thirty years.

The requirements for funeral director far surpass those expected of Teach For America candidates, including

- Longer study of specialized content (twelve to twenty-four months for a funeral director; five weeks for a Teach For America candidate)
- More field experience (twelve to twenty-four months for funeral directors; zero months for a Teach For America candidate)
- More stringent internship requirements (twelve to twenty-four months for funeral directors; zero months for a Teach For America candidate)

Obviously, the job of a funeral director involves the acquisition of specialized knowledge and extensive experience working in the field prior to full-time employment. Yet the profession of teaching requires no specialized knowledge and no experience prior to full-time employment?

CONCLUSION

Currently, the requirements for becoming a doctor, lawyer, plumber, and funeral director are exponentially more exacting than the requirements for becoming a teacher. Medicine, law, and mortuary science require specialized, postbaccalaureate course work, sometimes lasting years. They also require extended practicum experiences, passing scores on national exams, and close mentoring for beginning practitioners. Programs in medicine, law, and mortuary science typically employ several decision points where aspirants to the profession are assessed and judged. Candidates found wanting are dropped from the program.

Even plumbing requires specialized course work, extended practicum experiences, passing scores on exams, and a lengthy apprenticeship. In contrast, entry to the teaching profession in many states now requires no specialized course work, no practicum experiences, and no mentoring. Today, many teachers are neither assessed nor judged prior to their first day on the job. In teaching, almost no one gets dropped from a program, unless their check fails to clear the bank.

Chapter Seven

The Teachers We Need vs.
the Teachers We Have

We live in an era of linguistic manipulation. The phrase *highly qualified teacher*, conspicuous in the election platforms and ensuing legislation of presidents Clinton, Bush, and Obama, originally referred to the idea that every American child deserves a great teacher. Unfortunately, *highly qualified teacher* has lost its veracity.

Hundreds of thousands of teachers in America today are considered highly qualified, though they have never been prepared in the art and science of teaching, have never interacted with real children, and have never received guidance from an expert teacher.

Consider the organization that calls itself the American Board for Certification of Teacher Excellence (ABCTE). First of all, the ABCTE is a business, not a board; secondly, this business has nothing to do with excellence. Rather, the ABCTE is a profit-seeking enterprise that offers certification for a negotiable fee (one hundred dollars off with coupon). The ABCTE does not provide an education nor does it require prospective teachers to gain experience in a classroom. Rather, the ABCTE offers an expensive test, which it creates and which it alone evaluates.

The ABCTE, which has been voted into law as a legitimate avenue to teacher certification in nine states, could never emerge in countries such as Singapore or Finland, whose tight control over teacher preparation precludes the possibility that a business's profitability could supersede the best interests of children.

In the references for this book, you will find seemingly innocuous sources that sound like governmental agencies. The *National Center for Education Information*, for example, is close enough to the *National*

Center for Education Statistics to be its governmental cousin. In fact, the National Center for Education Information (NCEI) is an organization whose mission is to promote the expansion of alternative certification programs throughout the nation.

The NCEI advocates doing away with course work, field work, and university-based teacher preparation. Although course work, field work, and mentoring are expected of future doctors, lawyers, funeral directors, plumbers, and policemen, the NCEI does not consider such preparation necessary for prospective teachers.

The NCEI sponsors annual conferences on the myriad advantages of cheap-and-easy alternative certification programs and the evils of lengthy, intensive, university-based preparation. Incredibly, faculty from some Walmart-influenced campuses have started presenting papers at the NCEI's annual conventions, and attendance at their conferences has been on the rise.

Because the NCEI's perspective is obviously biased, data and reports promulgated by the NCEI must be viewed with great skepticism. Yet a close investigation of statistics about alternative certification published on the website of the U.S. Department of Education (2009a) reveals that much of the information has been provided by the NCEI.

The National Council on Teacher Quality (NCTQ) is another organization that promotes alternative certification while attempting to masquerade as an objective, research-focused agency. The similarity of the name *National Council on Teacher Quality* to the name *National Council for Accreditation of Teacher Education* (NCATE) is no coincidence.

Whereas the NCATE advocates rigorous standards for teachers, including a full-semester or longer of student teaching and challenging and relevant course work, the NCTQ advocates a student-teaching experience of a few weeks and limited course work. Unsurprisingly, the president of the NCTQ is an alternatively certified teacher who started the first alternative certification program in Maryland. Chester Finn, who sits on the board of directors of the NCTQ also happens to be the president of the ABCTE.

Thus two organizations (the NCEI and the NCTQ) that provide the federal government and state agencies with data on alternative certification are also dependent upon the continuing proliferation of alternative certification for their survival. Given this reality, it seems unlikely that either the NCEI or the NCTQ will ever have anything negative to say about alternative certification.

Let's review the facts. The chief executive officer of a business that provides alternative certification for a fee (Chester Finn of the ABCTE) is on the board of directors of the organization (the NCTQ) that provides the reports that promote the benefits of alternative certification. Not only has the federal government failed to launch an independent evaluation of teacher quality, it has relied upon the NCEI and the NCTQ to provide data about the quantity and quality of alternatively certified teachers.

When a wolf is appointed to guard the sheep, one must expect that casualties will be heavy. As teacher certification across the United States has gotten easier, quicker, and more profitable for the wolves, the sheep have started disappearing.

One would hope that the rationale upon which the alternative certification business empire has been built—that unprepared, inexperienced students with poor academic records are somehow superior to well-prepared, experienced teachers with stellar academic records—will eventually not stand. However, this is precisely the argument that has molded teacher-preparation policy in the United States since the late twentieth century.

American children deserve more. They deserve teachers with specialized training in teaching specific content to a particular age-group. They deserve to have teachers with diverse, extended experiences with teaching real children. They deserve teachers who will be mentored in their early years by expert teachers and PhDs who understand what it takes to be an effective teacher. They deserve intelligent, creative, empathetic teachers who can help them love as well as learn the material.

In the United States, it takes five to six years of work and study to be able to handle pipes and five to eight years of work and study to be able to handle dead bodies. But, it only takes five weeks, sometimes less, to become a teacher of children.

five to six years for pipes
five to eight years for the dead
five weeks for children

It is inconceivable that a country that has prided itself on equality and opportunity has relinquished control over the education of its children to unskilled, untrained strangers. At the beginning of the twenty-first century, it is to our shame that the education of our children has come to mean so little.

References

Achieve. 2007. *Creating a world class education system in Ohio*. Columbus, OH: Ohio Department of Education.

Alabama Department of Education. 2009a. *Alabama educator code of ethics*. rhs .rcs.k12.al.us/...%20Ethics%2009/Educator%20Code%20of%20Ethics%20 May%2009.pdf (accessed November 19, 2009).

———. 2009b. Website. http://www.alsde.edu/html (accessed October 30, 2009).

Alabama Department of Education Teacher Education and Certification Office. 2005. *General information regarding Alabama teacher certification*. Montgomery, AL: Alabama Department of Education.

———. 2007. *Summary of the alternative baccalaureate-level certificate approach*. Montgomery, AL: Alabama Department of Education.

Alaska Department of Education. 2009. Website. http://www.eed.state.ak.us/ TEACHERCERTIFICATION/ (accessed October 30, 2009).

Allen, M. 2003. *Eight questions on teacher preparation: What does the research say?* Washington, DC: Education Commission of the States.

American Association for Employment in Education. 2005. *Educator supply and demand in the United States: 2005 executive summary*. Columbus, OH: American Association for Employment in Education.

American Bar Association. 2007. *Annotated model rules of professional conduct*. 6th ed. Chicago: American Bar Association, Center for Professional Responsibility.

———. 2009. Website. www.abanet.org (accessed October 26, 2009).

American Board for Certification of Teacher Excellence. 2007. *A higher standard*. Washington, DC: American Board for Certification of Teacher Excellence.

———. 2008a. *Candidate handbook*. Washington, DC: American Board for Certification of Teacher Excellence.

———. 2008b. *Passport to teaching information kit*. Washington, DC: American Board for Certification of Teacher Excellence.

———. 2009. Website. http://www.abcte.org/teach/idaho (accessed November 19, 2009).

American Medical Association. 2008. *Code of medical ethics: Current opinions with annotations 2008–2009*. Chicago: American Medical Association.

———. 2009a. *Declaration of professional responsibility: Medicine's social contract with humanity*. http://www.ama-assn.org/ama/pub/physician-resources/medical-ethics/declaration-professional-responsibility.shtml (accessed October 30, 2009).

———. 2009b. Website. www.ama-assn.org (accessed October 26, 2009).

American University. 2009. *Teacher education programs: B.A. in secondary education*. http://www1.mfa.american.edu/te_ba_sec.cfm (accessed January 16, 2009).

Angrist, J., and J. Guryan. 2008. Does teacher testing raise teacher quality? *Economics of Education Review* 27 (5): 483–503.

Arizona State University. 2009. *Critical requirements and major maps*. https://webapp.asu.edu/eadvisor/MajorMaps.html?init=falseandnopassive=true (accessed January 15, 2009).

Arkansas Department of Education. 2007. *Rules governing the code of ethics for Arkansas educators*. arkedu.state.ar.us/.../static/.../Rules_for_Code_of_Ethics_for_PC.doc (accessed November 19, 2009).

———. 2009a. Website. http://arkansased.org/teachers/licensure.html (accessed May 30, 2009).

———. 2009b. Websites. http://www.ade.state.az.us/ and http://www.azed.gov/CERTIFICATION/ (accessed May 22, 2009).

Bergeson, T. 2007. *Educator supply and demand in Washington State: 2006 report*. Olympia, WA: Washington State Superintendent of Public Instruction.

Bobak, J. R., and M. Hiester. 2007. *Public, private and nonpublic schools: Enrollments 2006–07*. Harrisburg, PA: Pennsylvania Department of Education.

Boise State University. 2009. *Teacher education programs*. Website. http://education.boisestate.edu/teachered/programs.htm (accessed January 19, 2009).

Bowie, L. 2008. State's teacher shortage appears to be easing. *Baltimore Sun*, November 4. www.baltimoresun.com/news/education/bal-md.teachers04nov04,0,3781799.story (accessed November 6, 2008).

Brady, M. 2009. No dog left behind. *Education Week*, January 28. http://www.ctc.ca.gov/.

Buffett, W. 2002. *Warren Buffett on derivatives*. www.fintools.com/docs/Warren%20Buffet%20on%20Derivatives.pdf (accessed November 19, 2009).

California Commission on Teacher Credentialing. 2008. *Quick facts.* Sacramento, CA: California Commission on Teacher Credentialing.

———. 2009. Website. http://www.ctc.ca.gov/ (accessed June 1, 2009).

Center for the Study of Ethics in the Professions. 2009. *New Jersey Department of Education code of ethics.* http://ethics.iit.edu/indexOfCodes-2.php?key= 12_498_476&PHPSESSID=9464f1b31b1092f4e0712dec9374074e (accessed November 19, 2009).

Certification Standards and Practices Advisory Council. 1997. *Professional educators of Montana code of ethics.* bpe.mt.gov/pdf/Code%20of%20Ethics.pdf (accessed November 19, 2009).

Chait, R. 2009. *From qualifications to results.* http://www.americanprogress.org/ issues/2009/01/qualifications_to_results.html (accessed May 22, 2009).

Clotfelter, C., H. Ladd, and J. Vigdor. 2006. Teacher-student matching and the assessment of teacher effectiveness. *Journal of Human Resources* 41 (4): 778–820.

Colorado Department of Education. 2008a. *Alternative licensing program and the teacher in residence program comparisons.* www.cde.state.co.us/cdeprof/ Licensure_alt1_info.asp (accessed September 24, 2008).

———. 2008b. *To become a teacher through alternative licensing program.* www .cde.state.co.us/cdeprof/LIcensure_alt1_info.asp (accessed September 24, 2008).

———. 2008c. Webpage. www.cde.state.co.us (accessed September 22, 2008).

Colorado Department of Education Office of Professional Services and Educator Licensing. *Teacher and/or special services' provider induction program template.* Denver, CO: Colorado Department of Education.

Commonwealth of Pennsylvania. 2006. *Final report of the Governor's Commission on Training America's Teachers.* Harrisburg, PA: Commonwealth of Pennsylvania.

Connecticut State Department of Education. 2000. *Fact sheet #123: Types of certificates.* Bridgeport, CT: Connecticut State Department of Education.

———. 2006. *A superior education for Connecticut's 21st century learners: Five-year comprehensive plan for education 2006–2011, adopted by the Connecticut State Board of Education on January 3, 2007.* Hartford, CT: Connecticut State Department of Education.

———. 2007. *Connecticut code of professional responsibility.* www.sde.ct.gov/ sde/lib/sde/PDF/Cert/ethics/tchr_code.pdf (accessed November 19, 2009).

———. 2009. Website. http://www.sde.ct.gov (accessed May 1, 2009).

Connecticut State Department of Education Bureau of Educator Standards and Certification. 2007. *Connecticut code of professional responsibility for teachers.* Hartford, CT: Connecticut State Department of Education.

Connecticut State Department of Higher Education. 2009. *The alternate route to certification program information.* Bridgeport, CT: Connecticut State Department of Education.

Constantine, J., D. Player, T. Silva, K. Hallgren, M. Grider, and J. Deke. 2009. *An evaluation of teachers trained through different routes to certification.* Washington, DC: U.S. Institute of Education Sciences.

Dana, R. 2004. Easing the way to a teacher certificate. *Washington Post*, November 25.

Daniels, H., and S. Zemelman. 2004. *Subjects matter: Every teacher's guide to content-area reading.* Portsmouth: Heinemann.

Darling-Hammond, L. 2007. *Testimony before the House Education and Labor Committee on the re-authorization of No Child Left Behind.* http://ed.stanford .edu/suse/news-bureau/displayRecord.php?tablename=susenewsandid=332 (accessed May 23, 2009).

———. 2008. A future worthy of teaching for America. *Phi Delta Kappan: The Journal for Education* 89 (10): 730–33.

Darling-Hammond, L., D. J. Holtzman, S. J. Gatlin, and J. V. Heilig. 2005. Does teacher preparation matter? Evidence about teacher certification, Teach For America, and teacher effectiveness. *Education Policy Analysis Archives* 13 (42) http://epaa.asu.edu/epaa/v13n42/ (accessed May 23, 2009).

Delaware Department of Education. 2009. Websites. www.doe.k12.de.us and https://deeds.doe.k12.de.us/default.aspx (accessed July 4, 2009).

Derse, L. 2005. *Alternative certification programs in Wisconsin: Building on partnerships.* Paper presented at the National Center for Alternative Certification Second Annual Conference, Lake Buena Vista, FL.

Detroit Board of Education. 2008. *Detroit public schools 2008 adopted budget.* www.detroitk12.org/.../FY%202007-2008%20ADOPTED%20BUDGET-1. pdf (accessed November 19, 2009).

Dillon, S. 2008. Teach For America sees surge in popularity. *New York Times*, May 14.

District of Columbia State Education Agency. 2009. Website. http://www.osse .dc.gov (accessed March 2, 2009).

District of Columbia State Education Agency Office of Academic Credentials and Standards. 2005. *Directory of state approved educational programs.*

Driscoll & Fleeter. 2007. *Tables and figures for the 2007 condition of teacher supply and demand in Ohio.* www.ehhs.kent.edu/councils/teachered/.../COT SupplyDemand20072.pdf (accessed November 19, 2009).

Duncan-Poiter, J. 2006. *Update on alternative teacher preparation programs.* http:// www.regents.nysed.gov/meetings/2006Meetings/February2006/0206heppd3 .htm (accessed November 19, 2009).

Editorial Projects in Education Research Center. 2008a. *A special supplement to* Education Week's *quality counts: Arkansas.* www.edweek.org/media/ew/qc/2008/18shr.ar.h27.pdf (accessed November 19, 2009).

———. 2008b. *A special supplement to* Education Week's *quality counts: National highlights 2008: The teaching profession.* www.pewcenteronthestates.org/.../National%20Highlights%20Report.pdf (accessed November 19, 2009).

Education Commission of the States. 2003. Eight questions on teacher preparation: What does the research say? Washington, DC: Education Commission of the States.

Education Professional Standards Board of Kentucky. 2008. *Progress report on EPSB goals and strategies 2007–2008.*

Educational Testing Service. 2004. *Where we stand on teacher quality.* Princeton, NJ: Educational Testing Service.

Entwistle, N. 2004. Review of learning to teach in higher education. *Assessment and Evaluation in Higher Education* 29 (5): 643–44.

Feistritzer, C. E. 2005. *Profile of alternative route teachers.* Washington, DC: National Center for Education Information.

Finland Ministry of Education. 2009. Website. http://www.minedu.fi/OPM/?lang=en (accessed October 30, 2009).

Florida Department of Education. 2008. *New hires in Florida public schools: Fall 1998 through fall 2007.* Tallahassee, FL: Florida Department of Education.

———. 2009a. *The code of ethics and the principles of professional conduct of the education profession in Florida.* www.flboe.org/edstandards/pdfs/ethics.pdf (accessed November 19, 2009).

———. 2009b. Website. http://www.fldoe.org/edcert/ (accessed March 22, 2009).

Florida Department of Education, Florida Center for Interactive Media, and Florida State University College of Education Department of Educational Leadership and Policy Studies. 2008. *Beginning teachers from Florida teacher preparation programs: A report on state approved teacher preparation programs with results of surveys of program completers.* www.altcertflorida.org/.../Tchr%20Prep%20Report%2006-07%20-%20Exec%20Sum%205.pdf (accessed November 19, 2009).

Florida Department of Education Office of Research and Evaluation. 2008. *Critical teacher shortage areas: 2008–2009.* Tallahassee, FL: Florida Department of Education.

Florida State University Division of Undergraduate Studies. *Undergraduate academic program guide 2008–2009.* http://www.academic-guide.fsu.edu/ (accessed January 17, 2009).

Fox, J. 2009. Phil Gramm says the banking crisis is (mostly) not his fault. *Time,* January 24.

Gatlin, D. 2008. *Thinking outside of the university: Innovation in alternative teacher certification*. Washington, DC: Center for American Progress.

Georgia Professional Standards Commission. 2009. Website. http://www.gapsc .com/ (accessed April 5, 2009).

Goldhaber, D. 2007. Everyone's doing it, but what does teacher testing tell us about teacher effectiveness? *Journal of Human Resources* 52 (4): 765–94.

Grossman, P., K. Hammerness, M. McDonald, and M. Ronfeldt. 2008. Constructing coherence: Structural predictors of perceptions of coherence in NYC teacher education programs. *Journal of Teacher Education* 59 (4): 273–87.

Hawaii Department of Education. 2007. *Highly qualified teacher state plan.* http:// www.ed.gov/programs/teacherqual/hqtplans/index.html#hi (accessed November 19, 2009).

———. 2008. *Highly qualified teacher: Frequently asked questions.* December.

Hawaii Teacher Standards Board. 2009a. *Hawaii teacher standards board code of ethics.* ttp://www.htsb.org/html/details/teacherstandards/ethics.html (accessed November 19, 2009).

———. 2009b. Website. http://www.htsb.org/ (accessed January 2, 2009).

Hoffman, L., and Q. Shen. 2008. *Numbers and types of public elementary and secondary schools from the common core of data: School year 2006–2007.* Washington, DC: National Center for Education Statistics.

Hopkins, M. 2008. Training the next teachers for America: A proposal for reconceptualizing Teach For America. *Phi Delta Kappan: The Journal for Education* 89 (10): 721–25.

Horne, T. 2009. *2009 State of education.* http://www.azed.gov/administration/ superintendent/articles/2009StateofEducationSpeech.pdf (accessed February 26, 2009).

Howard-Jones, P. 2005. An invaluable foundation for better bridges: Comment. *Developmental Science* 8 (6): 469–71.

Howell, W. C. 1993. Moving to higher ground: A new era for training. *PsycCRITIQUES* 38 (2): 135–36.

Hughes, L. A. 2006. *Alternative routes to certification: Annual report to the Delaware Department of Education 2006–2007.* www.udel.edu/artc/documents/ 2006%20DOE%20Annual%20Report.pdf (accessed November 19, 2009).

———. 2007. *Annual report to the Delaware Department of Education: Alternative routes to certification.* Newark, DE: University of Delaware.

Idaho Department of Education. 2009a. *Code of ethics for Idaho professional educators.* www.sde.idaho.gov/site/.../PSC%20Code%20of%20Ethics%20 Booklet.pdf (accessed November 19, 2009).

———. 2009b. Website. http://www.sde.idaho.gov/site/teacher_certification/ (accessed February 24, 2009).

Illinois State Board of Education. 2007. *Educator supply and demand in Illinois: 2007 annual report.* Springfield, IL: Illinois State Board of Education.

———. 2009. Website. http://www.sde.idaho.gov/site/teacher_certification/ (accessed March 5, 2009).

Indiana Department of Education. 2009. Website. http://www.doe.in.gov/dps/welcome.html (accessed October 9, 2009).

Iowa Board of Education. 2009. *New Iowa elementary education PRAXIS II testing requirement.* http://www.iowa.gov/educate/index.php?option=com_docmanandtask=doc_downloadandgid=823 (accessed May 22, 2009).

Iowa Board of Educational Examiners. 2003. *Noticed rule.* http://www.iowa.gov/boee/newrules/not_rl111.html (accessed November 19, 2009).

———. 2008. *Licensure handbook.* Des Moines, IA: Iowa Board of Education.

———. 2009. Website. http://www.iowa.gov/boee/ (accessed January 29, 2009).

iteachTEXAS. 2009. Website. www.iteachtexas.com (accessed November 19, 2009).

Kansas State Department of Education. 2009. Website. http://www.ksde.org/Default.aspx?tabid=1648 (accessed October 20, 2009).

Kansas State Department of Education Teacher Education and Licensure, and B. Fultz. 2008. *Licensed personnel report state profile 2007–2008.* Topeka, KS: Kansas State Department of Education.

Kaplan University. 2007. Website. http://www.kaplan.com/aboutkaplan/newsroom/Pages/newsroom.aspx?ID=67 (accessed November 19, 2009).

Kentucky Education Professional Standards Board. 2006. *Professional code of ethics for Kentucky school certified personnel.* http://www.kyepsb.net/legal/ethics.asp (accessed November 19, 2009).

———. 2009a. *Progress report on EPSB goals and strategies, 2007–2008.* Frankfort, KY: Kentucky Education Professional Standards Board.

———. 2009b. Website. http://www.kyepsb.net/index.asp (accessed March 29, 2009).

Kinnunen, D. 2009. *Annual Report 2007–2008: Certificates issued and certificated personnel placements statistics.* http://www.k12.wa.us/certification/pubdocs/annrpt0708.pdf. (accessed November 19, 2009).

Larson, E., A. Hill, and D. Hirshberg. 2008. *Teacher supply and demand in Alaska—A 2005 snapshot.* www.iser.uaa.alaska.edu (accessed January 2, 2008).

Levine, A. 2006. Will universities maintain control of teacher education? *Change* (July/August): 36–43.

Liberty Science Center. 2009. Website. http://www.lsc.org/lsc/edprograms/profdev/gateway (accessed February 10, 2009).

Los Angeles Unified School District. 2009. *Teacher credentialing.* www.lausd.edu (accessed January 9, 2009).

Louisiana Department of Education. 2009. Website. http://www.doe.state.la.us/ Lde/tsac/home.html (accessed January 14, 2009).

Louisiana State University Department of Theory Policy and Practice. *Programs of study.* http://coe.ednet.lsu.edu/coe/ETPP/programs.html#secondk12fifth (accessed January 23, 2009).

Maine Department of Education. 2009. Website. http://www.maine.gov/ education/cert/index.html (accessed March 3, 2009).

Maine Regional Teacher Development Centers. 2008. *A plan to promote teacher quality and address Maine's teacher shortages.* Bangor, ME: University of Maine System.

Mangan, K. 2009. Medical schools should re-examine admissions and training methods, experts say. *Chronicle of Higher Education*, January 30.

Maryland Division of Occupational and Professional Licensing State Board of Plumbing License Requirements. 2009. Website. http://www.dllr.state.md.us/ license/plumb/plreq.htm (accessed October 22, 2009).

Maryland State Department of Education. 2009a. Website. http://www.maryland publicschools.org/msde/divisions/certification/certification_branch/ (accessed March 24, 2009).

———. 2009b. *Maryland approved alternative preparation programs.* http:// marylandpublicschools.org/MSDE/divisions/certification/progapproval/maapp _10_07.htm (accessed May 22, 2009).

Maryland State Department of Education Division of Certification and Accreditation Program Approval and Assessment Branch. 2006. *Proposal form for alternative teacher preparation programs.* Annapolis, MD: Maryland State Department of Education.

Maryland Teacher Shortage Task Force. 2008. *Maryland Teacher Shortage Task Force report.* http://www.marylandpublicschools.org/MSDE/divisions/ leadership/programs/tstf/ (accessed November 19, 2009).

Massachusetts Department of Elementary and Secondary Education. 2009a. *Regulations for educator licensure and preparation program approval.* http:// www.doe.mass.edu/lawsregs/603cmr7.html?section=all (accessed November 19, 2009).

———. 2009b. Website. http://www.doe.mass.edu/Educators/e_license.html ?section=k12 (accessed October 10, 2009).

Mathematica Policy Research. 2008. *Passport to teaching: Career choices and experiences of American board certified teachers final report June 11, 2008.* Washington, DC: Mathematica Policy Research.

Medina, J. 2009. Teacher training termed mediocre. *New York Times*, October 29.

Michigan Department of Education. 2008. *Michigan professional standards meeting: Committee notes.* Lansing, MI: Michigan Department of Education.

———. 2009. Website. http://www.michigan.gov/mde/0,1607,7-140-6530_5683_14795---,00.html (accessed January 9, 2009).

Michigan Department of Education Office of Professional Preparation Services. 2008. *Facts about teacher certification in Michigan.* Lansing, MI: Michigan Department of Education.

Michigan State Board of Education. 2008. *Reference manual.* Lansing, MI: Michigan Department of Education.

Michigan State University. *Secondary teacher preparation at Michigan State University.* http://ed-web2.educ.msu.edu/team4/ (accessed January 20, 2009).

Mid-continent Research for Education and Learning. 2003. *Teacher supply and demand in the state of Colorado.* Denver, CO: Mid-continent Research for Education and Learning.

Mid-continent Research for Education and Learning, R. Reichardt, B. V. Buhler, M. Akiba, and Colorado Department of Education Institute of Education Sciences. 2003. *Teacher supply and demand in the State of Colorado.* Denver, CO: Colorado Department of Education.

Minnesota Board of Teaching. 2003. *Code of ethics for Minnesota teachers.* https://www.revisor.mn.gov/rules/?id=8700.7500 (accessed November 19, 2009).

Minnesota Department of Education. 2005a. *Teacher supply and demand: FY 2004 report to the legislature.* Minneapolis, MN: Minnesota Department of Education.

———. 2005b. *Teacher supply and demand: FY 2005 report to the legislature.* Minneapolis, MN: Minnesota Department of Education.

———. 2007. *Teacher supply and demand: FY 2006 report to the legislature.* Minneapolis, MN: Minnesota Department of Education.

———. 2008a. *Acceptance of licensure programs from out of state and online teacher preparation programs for licensure.* Minneapolis, MN: Minnesota Department of Education.

———. 2008b. *Minnesota educator license application instructions and checklists.* Minneapolis, MN: Minnesota Department of Education.

Mississippi Department of Education. 2008. *Mississippi's alternate routes to educator licensure.* Jackson, MS: Mississippi Department of Education.

———. 2009. Website. http://www.mde.k12.ms.us/ed_licensure/ (accessed October 11, 2009).

Missouri State Board of Education. 2007. *2005–2006 report of the public schools of Missouri.* Jefferson City, MO: Missouri State Board of Education.

———. 2009. Website. http://dese.mo.gov/divteachqual/teachcert/ (accessed October 27, 2009).

Missouri State Teachers Association. 2009. *MSTA's code of professional ethics.* http://www.msta.org/about/codeofethics.aspx (accessed November 19, 2009).

Montana Department of Education. 2009. Website. www.opi.state.mt.us (accessed October 31, 2009).

Murnane, R., and B. Phillips. 1981. Learning by doing, vintage, and selection: Three pieces of the puzzle relating teaching experience and teaching performance. *Economics of Education Review* 1 (4): 453–65.

National Board for Professional Teaching Standards. 2006. *Improving teaching quality with Take One!* Washington, DC: National Board for Professional Teaching Standards.

National Center for Education Information. 2005. *Alternative teacher certification 2005*. Washington, DC: National Center for Education Information.

———. 2007. *Overview of alternative routes to teacher certification*. Washington, DC: National Center for Education Information.

———. 2008. *National center for alternative certification database*. Washington, DC: National Center for Education Information.

National Center for Education Statistics. 2004. *Teacher attrition and mobility: Results from the teacher follow-up survey, 2000–01*. Washington, DC: National Center for Education Statistics.

National Commission on Excellence in Education. 1984. *A nation at risk*. Cambridge, MA: USA Research.

National Commission on Teaching and America's Future, and Hawaii Policy Group. 2001. *The magic weaver: Securing the future for Hawaii's children*. Honolulu, HI: Hawaii Department of Education.

National Council for Accreditation of Teacher Education. 2009. *Professional standards for the accreditation of teacher preparation institutions*. http://www.ncate.org/public/standards.asp (accessed November 19, 2009).

National Education Association. 2009a. *Code of ethics*. http://www.nea.org/home/30442.htm (accessed November 19, 2009).

———. 2009b. Website. www.nea.org (accessed October 21, 2009).

National University. 2009a. *Bachelor's degree in single credential*. San Diego, CA: National University.

———. 2009b. *Master's in education degree program*. San Diego, CA: National University.

———. 2009c. *Take the first step today*. San Diego, CA: National University.

Nebraska Department of Education. 2008. *Issuances of certificate and permits to teach, provide special services, and administer in Nebraska schools: Title 92, Chapter 21*. Lincoln, NE: Nebraska Department of Education.

———. 2009. Website. http://www.nde.state.ne.us/tcert/ (accessed October 30, 2009).

Nebraska Professional Practices Commission. 1967. *Code of ethics, teaching profession, state of Nebraska, standards of professional practices*. nppc.nol.org/ethics.pdf (accessed November 19, 2009).

Nevada State Board of Education. 2009. Website. www.doe.nv.gov/ (accessed February 6, 2009).

New Hampshire Department of Education. 2009. Website. http://www.ed.state.nh.us/education/beEd.htm (accessed October 2, 2009).

New Hampshire Department of Education Division of Program Support, prepared by N. C. Smith, and K. J. Mackin. 2006. *Report on New Hampshire educators: Credentialing and employment trends*. Concord, NH: New Hampshire Department of Education.

New Jersey Department of Education. 2009a. *New Jersey licensure and credentials*. http://www.nj.gov/education/educators/license/provprogram.htm (accessed February 2, 2009).

———. 2009b. Website. http://www.nj.gov/education/educators/license/ (accessed April 2, 2009).

New Jersey Department of Education Office of Licensure and Credentials. 2009. *Guide to certification in New Jersey 2008–09*. Trenton, NJ: New Jersey Department of Education.

New Mexico Public Education Department. 2007. *Requirements and guidelines for the preparation of the New Mexico online resources for learning, portfolio for alternative licensure*. Albuquerque, NM: New Mexico Public Education Department.

———. 2009. Website. http://www.ped.state.nm.us/licensure/ (accessed October 20, 2009).

New York State Education Department. 2009a. *New York State code of ethics for educators*. http://www.highered.nysed.gov/tcert/resteachers/codeofethics.html#statement (accessed November 19, 2009).

———. 2009b. Website. http://www.nysed.gov/ (accessed October 19, 2009).

New York State Teacher Quality Research Center Pilot Project. 2008. *Where were New York City's 2005–2006 first-year teachers prepared?* New York: New York State Education Department.

North Carolina Department of Instruction. 2009. Website. http://www.dpi.state.nc.us/licensure/ (accessed October 21, 2009).

North Dakota Educational Practices and Standards Board. 2009. Website. http://www.nd.gov/espb/ (accessed March 13, 2009).

North Dakota State University Graduate School of Education. 2009. http://www.ndsu.edu/gradschool/about_us/graduate_programs/education/ (accessed January 28, 2009).

Office of the State Superintendent of Education Office of Educator Licensing and Accreditation. 2008. *Directory of State Approved Educational Programs*.

Ohio Department of Education. 2009. Website. www.ode.state.oh.us (accessed October 31, 2009).

Ohio State University College of Education and Human Ecology. 2009. Website. http://ehe.osu.edu/ (accessed January 28, 2009).

Oklahoma Department of Education. 2008a. *Application for Oklahoma school certificate.* Oklahoma City, OK: Oklahoma Department of Education.

———. 2008b. *Application for Oklahoma school license.* Oklahoma City, OK: Oklahoma Department of Education.

———. 2008c. *Certification guide for school staff assignments.* Oklahoma City, OK: Oklahoma Department of Education.

———. 2008d. *National Board Certification Day: 2006–2007 certification report.* Oklahoma City, OK: Oklahoma Department of Education.

———. 2008e. *Oklahoma Department of Education 2006–2007 facts.* sde.state .ok.us/services/data/statcard.html (accessed September 2, 2008).

Oklahoma State Department of Education Professional Services Division. 2008. *Certification guide for school staff assignments: July 2008.*

Oklahoma State Regents for Higher Education. 2002. *Teacher supply and demand study.* http://www.okhighered.org/studies-reports/teach-supply/ (accessed September 2, 2008).

Oregon Teacher Standards and Practices. 2009. Website. http://www.tspc.state .or.us (accessed October 20, 2009).

Oregon University System. 2006. *How to become an Oregon teacher: An advising guide to teacher preparation programs in the state of Oregon.* www.ous .edu/teachedguide.htm (accessed February 2, 2008).

Pennsylvania Department of Education. 2009. Website. http://www.teaching .state.pa.us/teaching/site/default.asp (accessed October 16, 2009).

Pennsylvania State University. 2008. *University bulletin: Undergraduate degree programs.* http://bulletins.psu.edu/bulletins/bluebook/print_college_campus .cfm?id=26 (accessed January 28, 2009).

Professional Educator Standards Board. 2009. *Standard V.* www.pesb.wa.gov/ ProgramReview/documents/StandardV.pdf (accessed November 19, 2009).

Professional Standards and Practices Commission. 1992. *Chapter 235. Code of professional practice and conduct for educators.* http://www.pacode.com/ secure/data/022/chapter235/chap235toc.html (accessed November 19, 2009).

Professional Standards Board. 2009. *The Professional Standards Board's ethical guideline for Delaware educators.* www.doe.k12.de.us/csa/profstds/files/ PSBEthicalGuidelineFinal8609.pdf (accessed November 19, 2009).

Professional Standards Council, and Teacher Education Professional Development and Licensing Team. 2007. *2006–2007 annual report.* dpi.wi.gov/Tepdl/ pdf/tepdlpscreport07.pdf (accessed November 19, 2009).

Program for International Student Achievement. 2007. *PISA 2006: Science competencies for tomorrow's world.* Paris: Organization for Economic Cooperation and Development.

———. 2009. *Bright country Finland.* http://www.pisa2006.helsinki.fi/finnish_school/educational_system/teacher_training.htm (accessed October 30, 2009).

Public Agenda. 2007. *Lessons learned: New teachers talk about their jobs, challenges and long-range plans.* Washington, DC: Public Agenda.

Rado, D. 2009. Many are called, but few chosen to teach: North Shore schools districts say they have far more applications from newly minted educators than job openings available. Chicagotribune.com (accessed February 4, 2009).

Rampell, C. 2009. How much do doctors in other countries make? *New York Times*, July 15. economi.blogs.nytimes.com/2009/07/15/how-much-do-doctors-in-other-countries-make/ (accessed October 16, 2009).

Region One Education Service Center. 2009. www.esc1.net. (accessed April 3, 2009).

Remaley, M. H. 2008. Teachers challenge: Diverse 21st century class. *Newsday.com* (accessed September 2, 2008).

Rhode Island Department of Elementary and Secondary Education. 2004. *Non-traditional certification program guidelines: Adopted by Board of Regents February 12, 2004.* Providence, RI: Rhode Island Department of Elementary and Secondary Education.

———. 2008a. *Rhode Island aspiring teachers pilot program: Application package.* Providence, RI: Rhode Island Department of Elementary and Secondary Education.

———. 2008b. *Rhode Island instructions for renewal.* Providence, RI: Rhode Island Department of Elementary and Secondary Education.

———. 2008c. *Mentor program.* Providence, RI: Rhode Island Department of Elementary and Secondary Education.

———. 2009. *Rhode Island educator code of professional responsibility.* http://www.rifthp.org/files/uploads/RICodeofResponsibility0809.pdf (accessed November 19, 2009).

Ricciardelli, M. 2009. Top 20 lobby expenditures equals over 1 billion dollars in the last 2 1/2 years. *Health Reform Watch: A Web Log of the Seton Hall University School of Law, Health Law and Policy Program.* http://www.healthreformwatch.com/2009/08/05/top-20-lobby-expenditures-equals-over-1-billion-dollars-in-the-last-2-12-years/ (accessed October 30, 2009).

Rivkin, S., E. Huanushek, and J. Kain. 2005. Teachers, schools, and academic achievement. *Econometrica* 73 (2): 417–58.

Roach, R. 2003. Going online with MARCO: Maryland initiative expedites certification process for new teachers. *Black Issues in Higher Education*, April 24. http://findarticles.com/p/articles/mi_m0DXK/is_5_20/ai_101413768/ (accessed November 19, 2009).

Rutgers University. 2009. *New Jersey Graduate School of Education: Becoming a teacher.* http://www.gse.rutgers.edu/decisiontree/genDecisionTreeTeacherUndergrad.asp (accessed January 25, 2009).

Sawchuk, S. 2009. Growth model. *Education Week* 29 (3): 27–29.

Sclafani, S. 2008. *Rethinking human capital in education: Singapore as a model for teacher development.* Washington, DC: Aspen Institute.

Section 37-3-2 Nontraditional Teacher Preparation Internship Programs. 2009. http://board.mde.k12.ms.us/SBE_December_2006/Tab%2023%20-%20EL%20-%20backup%20-%20Nontraditional%20Teacher%20&%20Educator%20Preparation%20Report.pdf (accessed November 19, 2009).

Shanmugaratnam, T. 2006. *Speech by Mr. Tharman Shanmugaratnam, Minister for Education and Second Minister for Finance, at the MOE Workplan Seminar 2006, on Wednesday, 28 September 2006 at 10.00 AM at the Ngee Ann Polytechnic Convention Centre.* http://www.moe.gov.sg/speeches/2006/sp20060928.htm (accessed November 19, 2009).

South Carolina Department of Education. 2009. *Educator quality and leadership.* Website. http://www.scteachers.org/ (accessed November 19, 2009).

South Carolina Division of Educator Quality and Leadership. 2006. *Education in South Carolina: Quick facts.* Columbia, SC: South Carolina Division of Educator Quality and Leadership.

South Carolina State Board of Education. 2008. *Annual report on individuals who have applied for certification in South Carolina based on qualifying for the Passport to Teaching Certificate through the American Board for Certification of Teacher Excellence (ABCTE).* Columbia, SC: South Carolina State Board of Education.

South Dakota Department of Education. 2008. *Code of professional ethics for teachers.* http://doe.sd.gov/oatq/propractices/PTPSC/ethicsteach.asp (accessed November 19, 2009).

———. 2009. Website. http://doe.sd.gov/oatq/teachercert/ (accessed September 25, 2009).

South Dakota State University. *Teacher education.* http://www3.sdstate.edu/Academics/CollegeOfEducationAndCounseling/TeacherEducation/Index.cfm (accessed January 29, 2009).

South Florida Community College Educator Preparation Institute. 2007. *General information 2007–2008.* Avon Park, FL: South Florida Community College.

South Texas College. 2009. *Alternative certification program.* www.admin.southtexascollege.edu. (accessed October 1, 2008).

Starr, P. 1982. *The social transformation of American medicine.* New York: Basic Books.

State Board for Educator Certification. 2002. *Proposed code of ethics and standard practices for Texas educators.* www.sbec.state.tx.us/sbeconline/brdinfo/agendas/2002_03/d10_att2.pdf (accessed November 19, 2009).

——. 2009. Website. http://www.sbec.state.tx.us/SBECOnline/certinfo/becometeacher.asp (accessed April 1, 2009).

St. Joseph's University Learning Institute. 2008. *Course offerings for fall 2008.* http://www.sju.edu/academics/centers/learninginstitute/fall.html (accessed August 27, 2008).

Strauss, V. 2008. Hundreds linked to diploma mill. *Washington Post*, July 31.

Teacher Distribution Project Steering Team. 2007. *Wisconsin Teacher Distribution Project report executive summary, prepared for the Wisconsin Department of Public Instruction.* Madison, WI: Wisconsin Department of Public Instruction.

Teach For America. 2009. Website. www.teachforamerica.org/about/regions/dc_region.htm (accessed February 9, 2009).

Tennessee Department of Education. 2008a. *Adding an additional degree.* www.state.tn.us.education/lic/add.shtml (accessed October 2, 2008).

——. 2008b. *Tennessee Department of Education report card 2007.* www.edu.repoortcard.state.tn.us (accessed October 1, 2008).

——. 2008c. *Tennessee licensure standards and induction guidelines.* Nashville, TN: Tennessee Department of Education.

Tennessee State Board of Education. 2006. *Agenda action item: IV.B. November 3, 2006—Alternative preparation for licensure policy.* Nashville, TN: Tennessee Department of Education.

Texas Association of School Administrators, and Superintendent Participants in the Public Education Visioning Institute. 2008. *Creating a new vision for public education in Texas: A work in progress for conversation and further development.* Austin, TX: Public Education Visioning Institute.

Texas Higher Education Coordinating Board. 2007a. *Teacher production by certification area—Longitudinal certification count, statewide by program 2006–2007.* Austin, TX: Texas Higher Education Coordinating Board.

——. 2007b. *Teacher production by certification area—Certification count by program and organization 2006–2007: Alternative program.* Austin, TX: Texas Higher Education Coordinating Board.

——. 2007c. *Teacher production by certification area—Certification count by program and organization 2006–2007: Standard program.* Austin, TX: Texas Higher Education Coordinating Board.

Texas Public Education Information Resource. 2007. *Teacher production by certification area—Longitudinal certification count, statewide by program.* Austin, TX: Texas Higher Education Coordinating Board.

Transition to Teaching. 2008. Website. www.tent2t.com (accessed October 2, 2008).

Union County College Economic Development and Continuing Education. 2008. *Overview, new pathways to teaching in New Jersey: An alternative route to teacher certification programs.* Cranford, NJ: Union County College.

United Nations Educational, Scientific and Cultural Organization. 2007. *State of teacher education in the Asia-Pacific region.* http://www.unescobkk.org/ fileadmin/template2/apeid/Documents/status_of_teachers/Singapore.pdf (accessed November 19, 2009).

University of Alabama at Birmingham. 2009a. *Secondary mathematics proposed program of study.* http://www.catalog.uab.edu/four_year_plans/Education/ Secondary_ED_Mathematics.pdf (accessed January 15, 2009).

———. 2009b. *2008–2009 undergraduate catalog.* http://www.catalog.uab.edu/ (accessed January 15, 2009).

University of Alaska at Anchorage. 2009. *College of Education.* http://coe.uaa .alaska.edu/programs/teaching/secondary/timelines/two-year.cfm (accessed January 15, 2009).

University of Arkansas. 2009. *Graduate catalog 2008–2009.* http://catalogof studies.uark.edu/08-010-GradCatalogCombined.pdf (accessed January 15, 2009).

University of California at Berkeley Graduate School of Education. 2009a. *Master's and Credential in Science and Mathematics Education* (*MACSME*). http://www-gse.berkeley.edu/program/macsme/macsme.html (accessed January 16, 2009).

———. 2009b. *Muse: Multicultural urban secondary education.* http://www-gse .berkeley.edu/program/macsme/macsme.html (accessed January 16, 2009).

University of California Linguistic Minority Research Institute. 2008. *California Dropout Research Project, statistical brief 10: What happened to dropouts from the high school class of 2004?* Santa Barbara, CA: University of California.

University of Colorado at Boulder School of Education. 2009. *Initial teacher licensure.* http://www.colorado.edu/education/prospective/teachereducation. html (accessed January 16, 2009).

University of Connecticut Neag School of Education. 2009. *Teacher education: The Integrated Bachelor's/Master's Teacher Education Program.* http://www .education.uconn.edu/departments/teachered/IBM.cfm (accessed January 16, 2009).

University of Delaware. 2009. *Secondary education.* http://www.udel.edu/ secondaryed/ (accessed February 20, 2009).

University of Georgia College of Education. 2009a. *B.S.Ed. in secondary English education program requirements.* http://www.coe.uga.edu/lle/english/secondary/bsed/requirements.html (accessed January 17, 2009).

————. 2009b. *Mathematics education: Teaching field — BSEd students.* http://www.coe.uga.edu/mse/math/programs/teaching.html (accessed January 18, 2009).

University of Hawaii at Manoa. 2009. *Institute for Teacher Education 2008–2009 catalog.* http://www.catalog.hawaii.edu/schoolscolleges/education/ite.htm (accessed January 18, 2009).

University of Illinois at Champaign Urbana. 2009a. *Course information suite programs of study: English.* http://courses.illinois.edu/cis/2008/fall/programs/undergrad/las/english.html#english (accessed January 19, 2009).

————. 2009b. *Course information suite programs of study: Mathematics.* http://courses.illinois.edu/cis/2008/fall/programs/undergrad/las/math.html#math (accessed January 20, 2009).

University of Indiana at Bloomington School of Education. 2009. *Office of Teacher Education program sheets.* http://education.indiana.edu/ProgramSheets/tabid/5425/Default.aspx#el (accessed January 20, 2009).

University of Iowa College of Education. 2009. *Office of Teacher Education and Student Services.* http://www.education.uiowa.edu/tess/ (accessed January 21, 2009).

University of Kansas School of Education. 2009a. *Mathematics secondary 6–12 education.* http://soe.ku.edu/math-secondary-education-program/ (accessed January 22, 2009).

————. 2009b. *English secondary 6–12 education.* http://soe.ku.edu/english-secondary-education-program/ (accessed January 22, 2009).

University of Maine at Orono College of Education and Human Development. 2009. *Secondary education: Program description.* http://factsheets.umaine.edu/EDHD/5-SED.pdf (accessed January 23, 2009).

University of Maryland College of Education. 2009. *Office of Student Services: Undergraduate student forms.* http://www.education.umd.edu/studentinfo/undergrad_forms/ugforms.html#progsheets (accessed January 24, 2009).

University of Massachusetts at Amherst School of Education. 2009. *Guide to educator licensure programs.* http://www.umass.edu/education/licensure/programs.shtml (accessed January 20, 2009).

University of Minnesota Twin Cities College of Education and Human Development. 2009. *Fields of study/major.* http://cehd.umn.edu/fields/Default.html (accessed January 20, 2009).

University of Mississippi College of Education. 2009. *Catalog: 2008–2009 academic year programs of study.* https://my.olemiss.edu/irj/portal/anonymous

?NavigationTarget=navurl://a3a79bf8082ded578833dc916e9f996e (accessed February 2, 2009).

University of Missouri at Columbia College of Education. 2009a. *College of Education bachelor of science in education, emphasis in mathematics education.* http://education.missouri.edu/TDP/files/hs_math.pdf (accessed January 22, 2009).

———. 2009b. *College of Education bachelor of science in education, language arts education.* http://education.missouri.edu/TDP/files/hs_english.pdf (accessed January 22, 2009).

University of Montana. 2009. *2008–2009 course catalog: Department of Curriculum and Instruction.* http://www.umt.edu/catalog/soe/curriculum_instruction .htm#secondary (accessed January 23, 2009).

University of Nebraska. 2009. *Undergraduate bulletin 2008–09.* http://www.unl .edu/unlpub/undergrad/downloads/ugb0809.pdf (accessed January 24, 2009).

University of Nevada Las Vegas Department of Curriculum and Instruction. 2009. *Undergraduate Secondary Teacher Education Program.* http://ci.unlv .edu/undergraduate/secondary (accessed January 25, 2009).

University of New Hampshire College of Liberal Arts Department of Education. 2009. *The M.A.T. and M.Ed. in elementary or in secondary education.* http:// www.unh.edu/education/index.cfm?ID=AE5602BFA03A-E5FE-876065189 30EEFE8 (accessed January 25, 2009).

University of New Mexico Teacher Licensure and Teacher Education Degree Programs. 2009. *Secondary education: Undergraduate advisement forms.* http://ted .unm.edu/advisement_forms_secondary_ug.html (accessed January 26, 2009).

University of New York at Albany School of Education Department of Educational Theory and Practice. 2009. *Teacher certification programs: Master of Science Secondary Education Program (MSSE).* http://www.albany.edu/etap/ graduate_programs/teacher_certification/MSSE.htm#guilding_principles (accessed November 19, 2009).

University of North Carolina at Chapel Hill School of Education. 2009. *Master of arts in teaching, M.A.T.* http://soe.unc.edu/academics/mat/pos.php (accessed January 27, 2009).

University of North Texas. 2009. http://www.untecampus.com/default.cfm?p= programinfoandPID=12 (accessed November 19, 2009).

University of Oklahoma College of Education. 2009a. *Requirements for the bachelor of science in education and certification in field of study: Language arts.* http://checksheets.ou.edu/langarts.pdf (accessed January 28, 2009).

———. 2009b. *Requirements for the bachelor of science in education and certification in field of study: Mathematics.* http://checksheets.ou.edu/mathmtcs.pdf (accessed January 28, 2009).

University of Oregon College of Education. 2009. *Licensure and certification: Prepare for the middle/secondary level teaching license.* http://education .uoregon.edu/licensure.htm?id=14 (accessed January 28, 2009).

University of Rhode Island School of Education. 2009. *Undergraduate programs: Secondary education.* http://www.uri.edu/hss/education/undergrad/ secondary/default.html (accessed January 29, 2009).

University of South Carolina Department of Instruction and Teacher Education. 2009. *Secondary education programs.* http://www.ed.sc.edu/ite/ite/SecEd.asp (accessed January 29, 2009).

University of Tennessee at Knoxville College of Education Health and Human Services. 2009. *Department of Theory and Practice in Teacher Education: Secondary education minor.* http://web.utk.edu/~tpte/minor/secondary _ed.html (accessed January 29, 2009).

University of Texas at Austin College of Education. 2009. *Teacher certification: Certification levels.* http://www.edb.utexas.edu/education/programs/ certification/about/cert_levels/ (accessed January 30, 2009).

University of Utah at Salt Lake College of Education. 2009. *Department of Teaching and Learning: Undergraduate level teacher licensure programs.* http://www.ed.utah.edu/tandl/Programs/Secondary-Licensure/ugrad -secondaryprogram.html (accessed February 1, 2009).

University of Vermont College of Education and Social Services. 2009. *Secondary education program.* http://www.uvm.edu/~doe/secondary/ (accessed February 1, 2009).

University of Virginia. 2009. *Curry School of Education.* http://curry.edschool. virginia.edu/ (accessed February 1, 2009).

University of Washington College of Education. 2009. *Academic areas and divisions: Secondary TEP.* http://education.washington.edu/areas/tep/secondary/ index.html (accessed February 1, 2009).

University of Wisconsin at Madison School of Education. 2009. *Teacher preparation.* http://www.education.wisc.edu/teacherprep/ (accessed February 2, 2009).

University of Wyoming at Laramie College of Education. 2009. *Program sheets for majors.* http://ed.uwyo.edu/majors.asp (accessed February 2, 2009).

Unmouth, K. 2008. State pushes for stricter rules on alternative certification teacher programs. *Dallas Morning News*, June 22.

U.S. Department of Education. 2009a. *Innovations in education: Alternative routes to teacher certification.* http://www.ed.gov/admins/tchrqual/recruit/ altroutes/index.html (accessed November 19, 2009).

——. 2009b. *Projections of education statistics to 2017.* Washington, DC: U.S. Department of Education.

———. 2009c. *Title II database.* www.title2.gov (accessed December 2007 to November 2009).

U.S. Department of Education Higher Education Act Title II Reporting System. 2005a. *Characteristics of alternative routes to teacher certification, by state: 2005.* Washington, DC: U.S. Department of Education.

———. 2005b. *Requirements for initial teaching certification or licensure: 2005.* Washington, DC: U.S. Department of Education.

U. S. Department of Education National Center for Education Evaluation and Regional Assistance. 2009. *An evaluation of teachers trained through different routes to certification.* Washington, DC: U.S. Department of Education.

U.S. Department of Education Title II Higher Education Act. 2008. *State reports 2008* https://title2.ed.gov (accessed January 2009 to October 2009).

Utah State Board of Education. 2009. *Utah educator standards.* http://www.rules.utah.gov/publicat/code/r277/r277-515.htm (accessed November 19, 2009).

Utah State Office of Education, prepared by S. Dickson. 2008a. *Education Interim Committee teacher quality report: Preparing, supporting and sustaining high quality educators for all students.* Salt Lake City, UT: Utah State Office of Education.

———. 2008b. *Public education: Fingertip facts 2008.* Salt Lake City, UT: Utah State Office of Education.

Vermont Board of Education. 2006. *2006–2007 strategic plan.* Montpelier, VT: Vermont Department of Education.

Vermont Department of Education. 2003. *Five standards for Vermont educators: A vision for schooling.* education.vermont.gov/new/pdfdoc/...prostandards/.../five_standards_03.pdf (accessed November 19, 2009).

———. 2006. *How are the children? A step toward transformation of education in Vermont.* Montpelier, VT: Vermont Department of Education.

———. 2008a. *Transformation of education in Vermont.* Montpelier, VT: Vermont Department of Education.

———. 2008b. *Vermont secondary schools for the 21st century.* Montpelier, VT: Vermont Department of Education.

———. 2009a. *Code of professional ethics and rules of professional conduct.* www.education.vt.gov/new/./educ_5500_licensing_ethics_code.pdf (accessed November 19, 2009).

———. 2009b. *Five standards for Vermont educators.* Montpelier, VT: Vermont Department of Education.

———. 2009c. *The Vermont re-licensing process.* Montpelier, VT: Vermont Department of Education.

——. 2009d. *VSBPE policy manual.* Montpelier, VT: Vermont Department of Education.

Virginia Board of Education. 2007. *Virginia licensure renewal manual.* Richmond, VA: Virginia Board of Education.

——. 2008a. *Annual report on the condition and needs of public schools in Virginia, presented to the governor and the general assembly November 20, 2008.* Richmond, VA: Virginia Board of Education.

——. 2008b. *Routes to licensure in Virginia.* http://www.doe.virginia.gov/VDOE/newvdoe/licroute.pdf (accessed January 17, 2009).

Virginia Department of Education. 2007. *Licensure regulations for school personnel effective September 21, 2007* http://www.doe.virginia.gov/VDOE/Compliance/TeacherED/nulicvr.pdf (accessed January 17, 2009).

Wachdorf, H. 2007. Teach for America on a path to growth in New Mexico. *New Mexico Business Weekly,* January 19. http://albuquerque.bizjournals.com/albuquerque/stories/2007/01/22/focus1.html (accessed October 1, 2009).

Wayne State University College of Education. 2009. *Alternative teacher certification: Limited license to instruct.* Detroit, MI: Wayne State University College of Education.

Wei, R. C., L. Darling-Hammond, A. Andree, N. Richardson, S. Orphanos, and School Redesign Network at Stanford University. 2009. *Professional learning in the learning profession: A status report on teacher development in the U.S. and abroad, technical report.* Stanford, CA: Stanford University.

West Virginia Department of Education. 2008a. *A chronicle of West Virginia's 21st Century Learning Initiative, 2004–2008.* Charleston, WV: West Virginia Department of Education.

——. 2008b. *Closing the achievement gap for 21st century learners.* Charleston, WV: West Virginia Department of Education.

——. 2009a. *Applications and forms: 37, 30, 4B, 20T, 8, 25, 25T, 12.* Charleston, WV: West Virginia Department of Education.

——. 2009b. *Employee code of conduct.* http://wvde.state.wv.us/policies/p5902.html (accessed November 19, 2009).

West Virginia Department of Education Office of Professional Preparation. 2005. *The quality of teacher preparation in West Virginia, August 2005.* Charleston, WV: West Virginia Department of Education.

West Virginia University College of Human Resources and Education. 2009. *Teacher education overview.* http://depts.hre.wvu.edu/hre/teachered/teachered.html (accessed February 1, 2009).

Wisconsin Department of Public Instruction. 2007. *Programs offering innovative/experimental or alternative routes to a Wisconsin license.* Madison, WI: Wisconsin Department of Public Instruction.

————. 2008. *Index of approved Wisconsin alternative programs leading to ini-tial educator license November 2008.* Madison, WI: Wisconsin Department of Public Instruction.

Wisconsin Department of Public Instruction Educator Supply and Demand Proj-ect. 2006. *Supply and demand 2006.* Madison, WI: Wisconsin Department of Public Instruction.

Worcester Public Schools. 2009. *District-based initial licensure program, Mas-sachusetts Department of Education approved initial licensure program.* Worcester, MA: Worcester Public Schools.

Wyoming Department of Education. 2008. *Wyoming education summary: A snapshot of Wyoming by the numbers: Fall 2008.* Laramie, WY: Wyoming Department of Education.

About the Author

Formerly the holder of the Judith Daso Herb Endowed Chair at the University of Toledo and the G. Leland Green Endowed Chair at Berry College, **Lawrence Baines** currently serves as the chair of instructional leadership and academic curriculum at the University of Oklahoma. For more on Lawrence Baines, see www.lawrencebaines.com. Up-to-date information on teacher quality may be found at www.teacherquality.info.